You Choose™ BOOKS

THE CIVIL WAR EXPERIENCE

AN INTERACTIVE HISTORY ADVENTURE

CAPSTONE PRESS
a capstone imprint

You Choose Books are published by Capstone Press,
1710 Roe Crest Drive, North Mankato, Minnesota 56003
www.capstonepub.com

Library of Congress Cataloging-in-Publication Data
Cataloging-in-publication information is on file with the Library of Congress.
ISBN 978-1-4765-0839-9

Photo Credits
Alamy: North Wind Picture Archives, 8, 95, 244; Art Resource, N.Y.: The Art Archive at Art Resource, N.Y., 169, © The Metropolitan Museum of Art, 143; The Bridgeman Art Library: © Chicago History Museum, USA/ Collins, J.A., 122, © Look and Learn/Private Collection, 214, © Look and Learn/Private Collection/Angus McBride, 180; Chamberlain and the 20th Maine by Mort Künstler, ©1993 Mort Künstler, Inc., www.mkunstler.com, 152, The Glorious Fourth by Mort Künstler, ©1989 Mort Künstler, Inc.,208; Classic Portraits in Oil/Noel Pantig, 196; Corbis, 116, 309, 312, 323, Corbis: Armstead and White, 282, Bettmann, 224, 318, Louie Psihoyos, 227, Royalty-Free, 210, 213; Cornell University Library/Division of Rare and Manuscript Collections, cover front and back (shackles), 238, 278; Gallon Historical Art, Inc., www. gallon.com (Texas Pride), 161; Getty Images, Inc: MPI, 183, 204, Stock Montage, 67; Hampton National Historic Site, National Parks Service, 265, 266; Library of Congress: Prints and Photographs Division: 13, 14, 16, 25, 33, 46, 48, 53, 58, 60, 63, 69, 72, 79, 81, 100, 107, 119, 149, 167, 233, 234, 254, 260, 286; The Louisiana Collection, State Library of Louisiana; Baton Rouge, 230; Louisiana State Museum, 241; Mary Evans Picture Library, 43, 102; Mendenhall Plantation: Rebecca G. Lasley, 297; National Archives and Records Administration (NARA), 22, 91, 92; North Wind Picture Archives, 127, 243, 257, 316; Ohio Department of Natural Resources, Parks and Recreation: Jim Glover, 247; Ohio Historical Society, 248, 251, 253, 272, 292, 294, 320; Ohio Historic Preservation Office: Annie McDonald, 304; Old Court House Museum, Vicksburg, Mississippi, 192; Painting by Don Troiani, www.historicalimagebank.com, cover (top), 40, 54, 87, 129, 134, 136, 162, 174, 177; Salem Historical Society, 300; Shutterstock: Scott Rothstein, cover (bottom); SuperStock, Inc: SuperStock, 105; Used with permission of Documenting the American South, The University of North Carolina at Chapel Hill Libraries, 189; The Virginia Historical Society, Richmond, VA (detail of painting Slave Auction), 275; www.printroom.com/ Legends of America, 144

Printed in the United States of America in Stevens Point, Wisconsin.
032013   007235R

In 1861, Southern men rushed to Richmond, Virginia, to volunteer for the Confederate Army.

Two railroads, the Manassas Gap and the Orange and Alexandria, meet at Manassas Junction. The railroads are a gateway to the Union capitol of Washington, D.C. They also lead to the naval shipyards at Norfolk, Virginia, and the federal arsenal at Harpers Ferry, Virginia.

You know that the army that controls the railroads will have a huge advantage. A battle can't be far behind.

➻ *To fight in the Confederate Army, turn to page **17**.*

➻ *To fight in the Union Army, turn to page **47**.*

➻ *To watch the battle as a civilian bystander, turn to page **73**.*

A huge number of weapons were made and stored at the U.S. Armory and Arsenal at Harpers Ferry, Virginia.

Early in the morning of April 12, 1861, Confederate cannons fired on Fort Sumter in South Carolina.

13

Turn the page.

TABLE OF CONTENTS

THE BATTLE OF BULL RUN:

AN INTERACTIVE HISTORY ADVENTURE

BY ALLISON LASSIEUR

CONSULTANT:
MARK SNELL, PHD
PROFESSOR OF HISTORY/DIRECTOR
GEORGE TYLER MOORE CENTER FOR THE STUDY OF THE CIVIL WAR
SHEPHERD UNIVERSITY

Table of Contents

ABOUT YOUR ADVENTURE

YOU are living in the United States in 1861. The country is fighting a civil war. Which side should you support? What will happen to you?

In this book, you'll explore how the choices people made meant the difference between life and death. The events you'll experience happened to real people.

Chapter One sets the scene. Then you choose which path to read. Follow the directions at the bottom of each page. The choices you make will change your outcome. After you finish one path, go back and read the others for new perspectives and more adventures.

*YOU CHOOSE the path
you take through history.*

Slaves provided the huge amount of labor needed to grow and harvest sugarcane and other crops in the South.

CHAPTER 1

A TORN COUNTRY

It's summer 1861. All over the United States, cities and towns are unusually quiet. You know it's not because of the hot weather. A few weeks ago, the Civil War began. No one is really sure what will happen next.

You're not sure why the war started, but you know it has something to do with slavery. For many years, white people in Southern states have owned black slaves. Slave owners say they need the slaves to work the plantations and farms that grow cotton, tobacco, and sugarcane.

9

Turn the page.

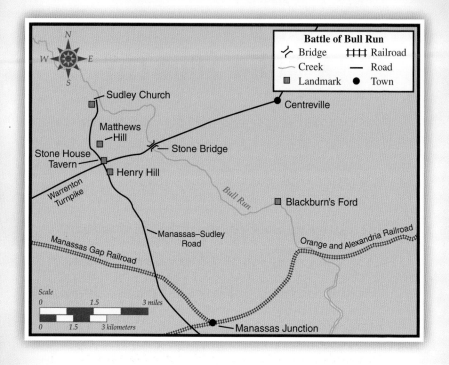

The map shows the Battle of Bull Run area with a legend containing: Bridge, Creek, Landmark, Railroad, Road, Town. Labeled locations include Sudley Church, Centreville, Matthews Hill, Stone Bridge, Stone House Tavern, Henry Hill, Warrenton Turnpike, Bull Run, Blackburn's Ford, Manassas Gap Railroad, Manassas–Sudley Road, Orange and Alexandria Railroad, and Manassas Junction. A compass rose shows N, S, E, W. A scale shows 0, 1.5, 3 miles and 0, 1.5, 3 kilometers.

10

Some people in Northern states think slavery is wrong. But many white Southerners say they have a right to do anything they want, including owning slaves. These Southerners believe the individual states should have the right to make their own laws.

The two sides have argued for years. In late 1860, Northern lawyer Abraham Lincoln was elected president of the United States. Lincoln was against the spread of slavery into the new western territories of the country. His election was the last straw for the Southern states.

One by one, seven states seceded, or withdrew, from the United States. Those states were South Carolina, Mississippi, Florida, Alabama, Georgia, Louisiana, and Texas. These states formed a new country called the Confederate States of America, or the Confederacy.

President Lincoln didn't believe the states had a right to secede. He vowed to make sure the United States stayed together, even if he had to go to war.

Turn the page.

On April 12, 1861, Confederate soldiers fired on Fort Sumter in South Carolina. U.S. soldiers in the fort surrendered the next day.

After the attack on Fort Sumter, Virginia, Arkansas, North Carolina, and Tennessee joined the Confederacy. Soldiers on both the Union and Confederate sides signed up to fight.

The Union Army includes about 35,000 men. The Confederate forces include the Army of the Potomac and the Army of the Shenandoah. Combined, these forces number about 32,000.

For weeks, the Union and Confederate armies have been moving toward Manassas Junction, Virginia. This village is about 30 miles southwest of Washington, D.C. You've never been to Manassas Junction, but you've heard it's an important place.

CHAPTER 2

FIGHTING FOR THE CONFEDERACY

It's dawn, and you're marching with your regiment. Last night, you boarded a train and left the Confederate capital of Richmond, Virginia. It's hard to believe that just a few weeks ago, you were working beside your father and brothers on your small Virginia farm.

When you heard about the attack on Fort Sumter, you rushed to enlist. Your family doesn't own slaves, but that doesn't matter to you. No Yankee government is going to tell you and other Southerners what to do.

Turn the page.

When you arrived at the Richmond capitol building, you were amazed at the crowds. All of the men in the county seemed to be there. Many of the young men in line were your friends.

One of the regiments forming will be part of the Army of the Potomac, commanded by General Pierre Beauregard. The other will be part of the Army of the Shenandoah, led by General Joseph Johnston.

→*To serve in the Army of the Potomac, go to page* **19**.

→*To serve in the Army of the Shenandoah, turn to page* **30**.

From Richmond, your regiment took a train to Manassas Junction. Now, you're camped along a nearby creek called Bull Run.

You and your fellow soldiers of the Army of the Potomac don't look much like an army. For one thing, no one has a real uniform. Like you, most men wear a wool jacket, cotton shirt, and wool pants. Your leather boots are nicer than the poor-quality shoes that some of the other soldiers wear. Your extra clothes and blanket are rolled up and tied together at the ends. You carry this blanket roll over your shoulder.

Some soldiers have bags called haversacks filled with food and ammunition. Everyone has a canteen to hold water, plus a rifle or musket and a bayonet.

Turn the page.

A soldier on horseback rides through camp. "General Beauregard is looking for brave men to work as couriers," the rider calls. "Volunteers should go to the general's camp at once."

"What's a courier?" you ask the soldier next to you.

"Couriers deliver messages on horseback during the battle," he replies. "It can be a dangerous job."

→ *To volunteer to be a courier, go to page* **21**.

→ *To stay with your regiment, turn to page* **25**.

You decide to be a courier. You walk to the general's camp on the grounds of a large farm. An aide sees you and motions to follow him.

"Who lives here?" you ask the aide as you reach a tidy farmhouse.

"Wilmer McLean," the aide replies. Inside the farmhouse, General Beauregard and several of his aides look at a map. Beauregard looks up. His dark eyes gleam with intelligence.

"So you want to deliver messages for me, eh?" he asks. You nod, suddenly nervous to be talking to the man who led the attack on Fort Sumter.

You're given a pistol and a fast horse. As you climb into the saddle, you hear the boom of distant cannons. The battle has begun.

Turn the page.

General Pierre G. T. Beauregard
was a native of Louisiana and a
Mexican War veteran.

Beauregard rushes from the farmhouse. "Courier," he shouts to you, "come here at once."

Beauregard hands you a piece of paper. "Take this to my commanders on the front lines." You nod, tucking the note into your jacket. Then you and your horse speed toward the cannon fire.

You don't go far before you hear the popping noise of gunfire. Smoke fills the air, making you cough. Bullets whiz past you. You bend low against your horse's neck and urge him forward.

Suddenly several Confederate commanders ride out of the smoke toward you. You pull the note from your pocket and hand it to the nearest one. He reads it quickly, scribbles a reply on the bottom, and hands it back.

Turn the page.

"Take this back to Beauregard at once," he orders. You decide to go back through the woods to avoid the gunfire. Soon you're completely lost. You finally see a clearing in front of you. The farmhouse at last, you think with relief.

You burst from the woods right into a regiment of Union soldiers. They are as startled as you are. You have just one second to make a decision.

➤*To run away, turn to page 27.*

➤*To open fire on the soldiers, turn to page 36.*

Blackburn's Ford on Bull Run
(shown in 1862) was the setting
for a skirmish on July 18, 1861.

You'd rather be an ordinary soldier. Your
regiment is positioned on Bull Run creek at an
area called Blackburn's Ford. The first thing you
notice is a terrible smell.

"What's that?" you ask, holding your nose.

Turn the page.

"A few days ago, there was a skirmish here between the Yankees and some of our soldiers. That smell is the dead bodies," a soldier tells you.

You notice several small mounds covered in mud and swarming with flies. You feel sick. To your shock, the order comes to bury the bodies. No one can stand to get too close. You and the other soldiers do little more than throw a few shovels of dirt on the bodies.

You barely finish when you hear the sound of guns and cannons firing. Your commander orders you to lie down. You don't understand why. The Yankees are coming. Shouldn't you get ready to fight?

➤ *To stand up, turn to page* **29**.
➤ *To follow orders, turn to page* **40**.

The Yankees recover from their shock and reach for their weapons. You barely have enough time to dash into the forest. Bullets thump into the trees beside you as you ride for your life. Finally, you make it back to the farmhouse. Right away, Beauregard sends you out with another message.

All afternoon, you dodge bullets and cannon fire as you deliver messages for the general. You and your horse are covered with soot and sweat. You both need water.

You stop at Bull Run. The creek water is brown with mud churned up by thousands of soldiers' boots. You're so thirsty that you don't care. You drop to your stomach and start slurping the water.

Turn the page.

After you drink your fill, you lie there panting. War isn't what you thought it would be. You sit up and look around. No one is here. You could easily slip away and go back to Richmond.

➤*To stay, turn to page* **37**.

➤*To desert the army, turn to page* **39**.

You enlisted to fight Yankees, not lie on the ground. You stand up, your hand on your rifle. Your commander sees you.

"Get down, soldier!" he yells at you. "Don't you know how to follow orders?"

You can't believe what the officer is telling you to do. What if he tells you not to move when the Yankees do show up to attack? You need to get out of here while you're still alive. Just then, the commander turns his back. Now is your chance.

Turn to page 39.

As you make your way to your regiment, you see General Johnston. You feel confident under his command.

Soon the orders come to march. The march across the rugged country is disorganized. Some units separate from the army and get lost. You wade through creeks up to your hips and trudge over steep hills. You never realized being in the army could be so miserable.

Early on the morning of July 21, your regiment arrives on the battlefield and gets into position. In the distance, you see the Yankees' guns shining in the sunlight. Someone shouts the order to attack, and you rush forward.

You and a few other soldiers drop behind a small mound. You start shooting at every Yankee you see. Soon the air is filled with smoke and the thundering sound of cannons and guns.

You keep loading and shooting. Bullets thump into the ground around you. One of the soldiers beside you slumps down, shot in the chest. You gulp and keep firing.

"Move position!" you hear. Without thinking, you jump up and run. In the confusion, you're separated from your regiment.

The morning turns into afternoon as you shoot, reload, and shoot again. When you run out of bullets, you grab more from the dead bodies scattered around the battlefield. You're thirsty, sweaty, and hungry. Your fingers are swollen and aching from loading and firing your gun again and again.

Turn the page

Ahead, you see a group of Confederate gunners being attacked. You rush to help them. One of the cannoneers appears through the smoke, a look of terror on his face.

"The other cannoneer is dead," he shouts. "I can't fire this alone. I need help." A company of Yankees is rushing toward you.

➻ *To help the cannoneer, go to page* **33**.

➻ *To attack the Yankees, turn to page* **45**.

Both Confederate and Union soldiers used cannons during the Civil War.

You drop your gun and help. You have no idea what to do, but the cannoneer shouts instructions. You load the cannonball and step back, covering your ears. A huge blast scatters the Yankees.

Turn the page.

As they run off, you look for the cannoneer. He's lying dead on the ground. You try not to think of him as you pick up your gun and rush back into battle. You need to find your regiment.

Soon you spot a few members of your regiment. They're running in the opposite direction from the battle.

"The battle is lost," one man shouts. "We're beat."

"The Yankees have won the day," another says over his shoulder.

Your heart sinks. If the battle is lost, there's no reason to keep fighting. Or is there? You haven't yet heard the order to retreat from a commander.

➼ *To run away, go to page* **35**.

➼ *To stay, turn to page* **42**.

From the looks of things around you, the soldiers are right. Confederate soldiers are streaming away from the battle, running for their lives. One even says that he heard a Yankee commander declare victory. The battle appears to be lost.

You feel discouraged. War isn't what you thought it would be. In the confusion, no one would know if you left the battle and went home.

Turn to page **39.**

You reach for your pistol and manage to fire one shot. But the Union soldiers are too fast for you, and there are more of them. Before you have a chance to fire again, a bullet rips through your chest. Your last thought is that you did your best to serve the Confederacy.

THE END

To follow another path, turn to page 15.
To read the conclusion, turn to page 103.

You decide to stay and fight. Before you can get up, a shadow passes over you. You're horrified to see that Union soldiers surround you.

The soldiers search you and find the message you are carrying. They also take your weapons, ammunition, and supplies.

"General McDowell will find this information very helpful," one of the Yankees says to you. "And you'll make a fine prisoner of war."

The soldiers push you forward. Soon you arrive at a Union camp. Several other Confederate soldiers are under guard. The Yankees laugh as they add you to the group of prisoners.

Turn the page.

You'll probably be sent to a prisoner of war camp in the North. You don't know what will happen to you, but you know your days as a soldier are over.

THE END

To follow another path, turn to page 15.
To read the conclusion, turn to page 103.

A patch of woods is nearby. You can hide there until you figure out where to go. When you reach the woods, you peek through the trees at the road. You see other soldiers running away. You feel guilty for leaving the army, but at least you're still alive.

As you plod down the road, the sounds of battle grow fainter. Finally, all you can hear is the steps of dozens of other tired, dirty soldiers who have deserted too. You're sick of war. You're going home.

THE END

To follow another path, turn to page 15.
To read the conclusion, turn to page 103.

The 4th Alabama Regiment fought on Henry Hill during the battle.

Dozens of soldiers get up and run, but you follow orders and remain on the ground. You and the rest of the regiment wait. And wait. You stay there all day, while the sounds of the battle come at you from all directions. That afternoon, you're at last given orders to move.

You cross Bull Run and move quickly down the road. Soldiers are shouting, "The Yankees are retreating!"

Great news! At first, you are ordered to prepare to attack the retreating Union forces. You grip your gun, ready to fight. Then the order comes to move back. You can't believe it, but you obey the order.

Finally, the news comes that the battle is over, and the Confederates won. You're happy about the news, but angry that you never fired a shot. There will be other chances, though. This is just the beginning.

THE END

To follow another path, turn to page 15.
To read the conclusion, turn to page 103.

You refuse to believe the news. With one last look at the retreating soldiers, you run back toward the battle.

Soon you come upon a small Confederate force near Henry Hill. You recognize their commander, General Thomas Jackson. You can see that Jackson's men are standing steady against the Yankee attack. You join them.

Right behind you is another Confederate brigade, commanded by General Bernard Bee. His hoarse voice rises over the sound of gunfire, shouting, "Look, men! There is Jackson, standing like a stone wall. Let us determine to die here, and we will conquer. Follow me!"

In no time, the combined forces are hammering away at the Yankee troops. Slowly, you push the Union Army back.

General Thomas "Stonewall" Jackson earned his famous nickname during the battle.

Turn the page.

You don't know how long you keep fighting. You can barely see through the smoke. At one point, a Union shot hits Bee in the stomach as he rides through the battle. But you and your fellow soldiers keep firing.

By late afternoon, there are no more Yankees to shoot. The battlefield is covered with the dead and wounded. You're not sure how you survived, but you did. You drain the last drop of water from your canteen as a rider gallops toward you.

"The battle is won!" the soldier croaks. "The Union is retreating. Victory is ours!" You sink to the ground in relief. Your army has won the battle. You hope it also will win the war.

THE END

To follow another path, turn to page 15.
To read the conclusion, turn to page 103.

You turn and yell as you fire at the oncoming Yankees. Just then, a sharp pain strikes you in the upper leg. You've been shot! Blood pours from your body as you sink to the ground. The last thing you see is the glint of the sun on the bayonets of the Yankee soldiers.

THE END

To follow another path, turn to page 15.
To read the conclusion, turn to page 103.

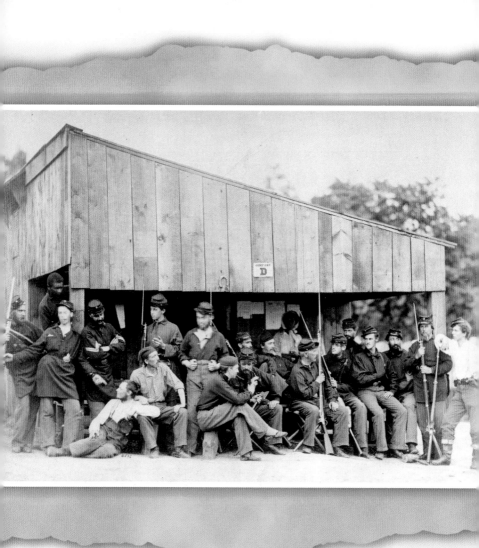

Union soldiers gathered at Camp
Sprague in Washington, D.C.,
before the Battle of Bull Run.

CHAPTER 3

DEFENDING THE UNION

You live in a small town in Michigan, where you work in your father's hardware store. You've never been more than 10 miles from home.

Your family is surprised that you want to enlist in the army after the attack on Fort Sumter. Your mother cries, "It's so far away. They don't need you." Father looks grim. But you are determined. Nothing is going to stop you from teaching those rebels a lesson.

Turn the page.

General Samuel Heintzelman led one of the five Union divisions at Bull Run.

You and all of your friends rush into town the next day to enlist. Before you know it, you are on a train to Washington, D.C. You know this is going to be the adventure of a lifetime.

When you arrive, you and your friends join General Samuel Heintzelman's Third Division. You've heard about Heintzelman's bravery in the Mexican War. You're looking forward to fighting under his command.

Washington, D.C., is nothing like you had imagined. The streets are muddy and filled with garbage. You and your friends spend two weeks practicing drills at camp. On July 16, your regiment gets orders to march toward Manassas Junction, Virginia. At last, you're going to war.

Turn the page.

Marching to war is much harder than you thought it would be. The few roads are narrow and pitted with holes. You trudge through scrubby fields filled with prickly thistles. At one point, you have to crawl across a log that forms a bridge over a deep ravine.

It takes your regiment three days to get to Centreville, a small town about 7 miles from Manassas Junction. You and your fellow soldiers set up camp near the town.

You're exhausted and hungry. So is everyone else. But the Confederate Army is out there, and you must be ready to fight. News comes that the army is dividing into several forces.

→*If your regiment attacks the Confederates'
left flank, go to page* **51**.

→*If your regiment heads toward the stone bridge
over Bull Run creek, turn to page* **60**.

General Heintzelman is planning a surprise attack on the left flank, or side, of the Confederate forces near Matthews Hill. As the Confederates march in rows, shoulder to shoulder, you'll attack them from their left. It won't be easy for the rows of soldiers to whirl around and face your attack.

To get to Matthews Hill, your regiment leaves the Warrenton Turnpike and scrambles north over a narrow, weedy path. After several hours, the path veers south. At Sudley Church, you get on the Manassas-Sudley Road.

Turn the page.

Near Matthews Hill, you're ordered to line up near a battalion of artillery. You see some soldiers dressed in colorful clothing.

"Who are they?" you ask the soldier next to you. He laughs.

"They're the Fire Zouaves, one of the most famous regiments in the Union Army," he says. "They're firefighters from New York City. I heard they helped put out a fire at the Willard Hotel in Washington, D.C., a few weeks back."

Before you have a chance to answer, you hear gunfire. The Confederates are attacking! You and the other soldiers drop behind a small hill and start returning fire.

Fire Zouaves wore a uniform of red shirts, short gray jackets, and baggy gray pants.

Turn the page.

The lack of standard uniforms made it difficult to tell Union and Confederate soldiers apart.

54

The heat of battle quickly surrounds you. Your ears ring from the boom of the cannons and the screams of pain from the wounded. A mixture of sweat, dirt, and gunpowder pours into your eyes, but you don't dare stop loading and firing.

You see a group of soldiers rushing toward you. It's hard to see through the smoke, but you think they're wearing blue uniforms. That doesn't help you, though. No one has matching uniforms. You have no idea if the soldiers are Union or Confederate. You feel something hit your leg, but you ignore the pain for the moment. You're too busy trying to decide what to do.

➤ *To wait to fire on the soldiers, turn to page 56.*

➤ *To fire on the soldiers, turn to page 57.*

As you hesitate, the soldiers raise their guns. Horrified, you realize that they're Confederates. You try to leap behind a tree, but the pain shoots through your wounded leg. You fall to the ground, bleeding. You pretend to be dead, hoping they'll leave you alone.

You lie still and try not to breathe as the Confederates search you. They take your rifle, your ammunition, and your food. You feel light-headed from the loss of blood.

Suddenly, you feel a lump beneath you. It's your pistol, which you shoved in your belt. You might be able to get to it.

→To grab your pistol, go to page 57.

→To continue lying still, turn to page 59.

You grab your pistol and open fire. A soldier in the front falls to the ground. To your shock, the rest turn and run. Relieved, you look down at the wound in your leg. Most of the bleeding has stopped, so you grab the shirt of a dead Confederate near you and wrap your leg. You also take his weapon and ammunition.

Your regiment has scattered, so you join a group of Union soldiers who are fighting near a small creek. You ignore the throbbing in your leg as you fire at the oncoming Confederates. You start to shake. When you try to walk, your leg buckles beneath you.

Turn the page.

The Stone House near Matthews Hill was used as a Union field hospital.

"That wound is bad," one of the soldiers says. "You need to get that looked at right away. There's a field hospital in the Stone House tavern not far from here."

You look around. The battle seems to have slowed down a bit. You might make it to the hospital. But you'd really rather keep fighting.

➤To stay and fight, turn to page **64**.
➤To go to the hospital, turn to page **66**.

Your trick works. The soldiers are too busy stealing your things to realize that you're still alive. With a final laugh and a kick to your side, they leave you. You lie there for a few minutes, trying to clear your head. When you finally sit up, you almost faint from the pain in your leg.

"Are you hurt, soldier?" a voice says. You look up to see a Union soldier you don't know. He's smeared with blood and dirt, just like you.

"That wound looks bad," he says. "Let's get you to a field hospital."

Turn to page 64.

The stone bridge over Bull Run was destroyed after the battle. It was later rebuilt.

The morning of July 21 is clear and warm. You and the other soldiers forget how tired you are as you march. Some of you stop to pick and eat wild blackberries.

Soon, you see a stone bridge. Thousands of soldiers are lined up there, ready to fight. You're ordered to move upstream from the bridge and cross the creek. From there, you march to an area called Matthews Hill.

A low roar is coming from ahead of you. There, the battle has been raging for hours. Cannons explode, shaking the ground. The yells and screams of the men mix with the sound of gunfire. You raise your gun and fire at the Confederate soldiers.

The air quickly becomes black with smoke and soot. It's hard to breathe. You cough, wiping dirt and sweat from your forehead. A bullet grazes the side of your head. Blood pours down your shirt collar. You don't have time to wipe it away as you keep shooting.

Behind you, a hoarse voice yells, "Move forward!" You can't tell who is speaking. You stop, trying to hear over the battle noise.

➤ *To obey the order, turn to page* **62**.

➤ *To wait, turn to page* **65**.

You scramble forward, yelling at the top of your lungs. Rebels scatter. The confusion of battle is all around you. It's hard to tell which soldiers are on which side. You just fire your gun and try to stay alive.

Sometime in the early afternoon, you hear news that makes your heart glad. The Union is winning! Sure enough, many Confederates are running away. It's not over yet, though. You'll keep fighting as long as the rebels keep coming. You shoot until you run out of bullets. For a moment, you panic.

Before you can move, an officer races up on horseback. "Fall back!" he yells. "General McDowell has ordered a retreat!"

You're stunned. "Sir, do you know why?" you ask him.

General Irvin McDowell was replaced as Union commander soon after the battle.

"The rebels have reinforcements on the way," he replies before galloping away.

There's no way you and the other tired Union soldiers can fight fresh troops. Large groups of soldiers turn around and begin an orderly retreat.

→To stay, turn to page **65**.

→To retreat, turn to page **67**.

You're not going to let a wounded leg stop you from beating the Confederates. But just as you raise your gun, you feel a sharp pain in your right leg. You've been shot in that leg too! As you fall to the ground, the other soldier catches you.

"You're going to the hospital now. No arguments!" he tells you sternly.

You know he's right. You can't fight with two wounded legs.

Turn to page 66.

You're determined to stay and fight. But as you raise your gun, you feel a sharp pain in your right leg. You look down to see the bloody bullet wound. Another soldier helps you stumble to Sudley Church, where the Union Army has set up a field hospital.

When you reach the church, you see wounded soldiers lying everywhere. Dead bodies are piled a short distance away. Your stomach churns.

A tired doctor in a bloody apron examines you. "Your bone is shattered," he says. "If I don't amputate this leg, you'll die."

➤*To agree to the amputation, turn to page 69.*

➤*To refuse, turn to page 71.*

The soldier helps you to the Stone House tavern. Someone binds your wounds with a dirty rag and gives you a sip of water.

You fall in and out of consciousness. When you wake up, it's early evening. The moans of the wounded fill the air. You call out, "What's happening?"

One of the wounded men replies, "It's a terrible day. The Confederates have won the battle. Worst of all, the army has left us here."

You fall back onto the filthy floor and close your eyes. It won't be long, you think, before the Confederates take you all prisoner. You wonder whether you'll still be alive by then.

THE END

To follow another path, turn to page 15.
To read the conclusion, turn to page 103.

Panicked Union soldiers thought the Confederates were chasing them.

You follow columns of soldiers as they leave the battlefield. Then you hear scattered gunfire behind you.

"The rebels! They're after us!" a voice shouts. The road is choked with wagons and civilians who have come out to see the battle. Panicked, the soldiers shove people out of their way.

Turn the page.

The soldiers break into a run, smashing into each other and turning over wagons and carts. You scramble out of their way. Somewhere in front of you is Washington, D.C., and safety.

After a while, you realize that the panicked soldiers were wrong. No Confederates are behind you. You walk all night. Every mile, you want to collapse, but someone grabs you and makes you keep going.

Late in the morning of the next day, you reach the outskirts of Washington. You collapse in a doorway. You vow to keep fighting for the Union. You may have lost the first battle, but you're determined not to lose the war.

THE END

To follow another path, turn to page 15.
To read the conclusion, turn to page 103.

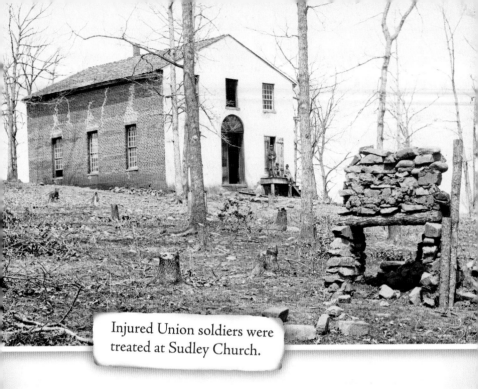

Injured Union soldiers were treated at Sudley Church.

You think for a minute, trying to ignore the pain. "Well, doc," you say finally, "I suppose I'd rather be alive with one leg than dead with two."

He nods. Another soldier grabs your arms and half-drags, half-carries you to the large tent behind the church. Several men are lying on blankets on the ground.

69

Turn the page.

You're lifted onto a wooden table. Another soldier puts a few drops of liquid on a cloth and then holds it to your nose and mouth. You fall unconscious.

Hours later, you start to wake up. You feel a searing pain in your leg. Someone puts a leather strap in your mouth. You bite down on it when the pain becomes unbearable. You look down to see a stump where your leg once was. You're in incredible pain. But at least you're alive.

THE END

To follow another path, turn to page 15.
To read the conclusion, turn to page 103.

There's no way you're going to let a doctor cut off your leg. "I'll take my chances, doc," you say stubbornly.

"I can't do anything for you, then," the doctor says. He gives you some medicine to help you sleep. Hours later, you awake in terrible pain. Your leg has become infected, and you are burning with fever.

As you float in and out of consciousness, you hear that the battle is over, and the Confederates won. You know you're dying, and you'll never know how the war ends.

THE END

To follow another path, turn to page 15.
To read the conclusion, turn to page 103.

In 1861, President Lincoln was sworn in as work was being done on the U.S. Capitol.

CHAPTER 4

WATCHING THE BATTLE

Washington, D.C., is an exciting city in 1861. Your family lives in a large home not too far from the U.S. Capitol. You've always had a comfortable life as the daughter of a successful businessman. Now, though, your world is shaken by war.

A few months ago, you heard the terrible news that Fort Sumter had been attacked. Most people laughed at the idea of the Confederacy. "This war will be over by the end of the summer," many people said. You're not so sure.

Turn the page.

The morning of July 21 is sunny and warm. You sit down to breakfast with your mother and father. The empty seat at the table reminds you that your older brother, Samuel, is gone. He enlisted in the Union Army right after the attack on Fort Sumter. His regiment marched off toward Manassas Junction a few days ago.

Everyone tries to be cheerful, but there is tension in the air. You pick up the newspaper and read about small skirmishes that have broken out between the two armies.

Father sees the look on your face and pats your hand reassuringly. "The war will probably be over by the end of the day," he says, smiling.

Mother agrees. "Those rebels don't have the stomach to fight," she says. But behind their calming words is a tone of fear.

There is a knock on your door. You're surprised to see your best friend, Abigail, and her younger brother, John.

"What are you doing out so early?" you ask.

"We're going out to watch the battle," Abigail says excitedly. "Father let us have the carriage, and we've packed a picnic lunch. Can you come with us?"

"Yes, do come," John adds. "It will be fun."

→ *To stay home, turn to page* **76**.

→ *To go with your friends, turn to page* **80**.

You hesitate. It would be exciting to see a real battle. But you're not sure that it would be safe.

"No, I don't think so," you say finally. "It's too dangerous. I don't want to get shot."

Abigail looks disappointed. "Mother made fried chicken. All of our friends will be there."

John nods. "Just come with us," he pleads.

But you're firm. Abigail and John climb into their carriage and drive away. You watch them go with a mixture of jealousy and fear. You don't want to go to the battle, but you don't want to be left out, either.

You climb to the small balcony on the third floor of your house and look down. You're surprised at the number of wagons and carriages on the road. More people are heading to the battle than you thought. You wonder if you made the right choice.

As it's Sunday, your family attends church as usual. It's hard to pay attention because everyone is whispering about the battle.

After the service, you and your family join other churchgoers gathered outside. Just then, your friend Elizabeth hurries past.

"Where are you going?" you ask her.

"My uncle works at the War Department," Elizabeth replies. "I'm going down there to see if there is news. Want to come with me?"

➤ *To go with her, turn to page* **78**.

➤ *To return home, turn to page* **85**.

The two of you head toward the War Department. When you arrive at the building, people are gathered near a side door. You and Elizabeth try to go in, but a guard stops you.

"Please tell us what's happening," you ask him.

"We're getting steady reports from the battle," one guard says. "The news seems good."

You and Elizabeth stay for several hours. You watch important-looking men bustle in and out all day. Every once in awhile, the guards tell you that the battle is going well.

Once, a very tall man in a black frock coat steps out. He has a tall hat perched on his head. You instantly know who he is.

"President Lincoln," you say as he passes you. "May God bless you today."

President Abraham Lincoln waited in Washington for news of the battle.

Lincoln stops and smiles at you. He reaches out to shake your trembling hand. "Thank you, young lady," he says. Then he climbs into a waiting carriage and rides down the street.

Turn to page 85.

Watching a battle sounds exciting, so you agree to go. You're surprised at the number of wagons and elegant carriages that fill the road. You and your friends happily wave and greet everyone you pass. It feels like you're going to a carnival.

You and your friends travel to the village of Centreville. A few dozen people have settled on a grassy knoll west of town to watch the battle. One man catches your eye. There's a large box strapped on his back.

You approach him curiously. "What's that?" you ask, pointing at the box.

The man smiles and shakes your hand. "I'm Mathew Brady," he says. "This is my camera equipment. I've come to record history."

Photo taken
July 22nd
1861

BRADY
The Photographer
returned from
Bull Run

Mathew Brady was the
most famous photographer
of the Civil War.

Turn to page 82.

You step back, suddenly shy. Mathew Brady, the famous photographer! "It's nice to meet you," you manage to tell him before you go back to your friends.

As you unpack the lunch basket, Abigail nudges you. She points to a large, dignified man sitting nearby.

"Do you know who that is?" she whispers. "That's Senator Henry Wilson of Massachusetts. He handed out hundreds of sandwiches to the Massachusetts soldiers as they marched into battle." You're impressed to be near such an important member of Congress.

It's not long before the echo of cannon fire fills the air. Excitedly, you stand up and peer through your opera glasses at the scene a few miles away.

Everyone else is standing up too. There's so much dust and smoke that you can barely see the troops moving toward the battlefield.

Soon your ears ache from the sound of the cannon fire. You still can't see the battle. By early afternoon, you are ready to go home. But Abigail and John aren't ready to leave.

"Let's get closer, so we can see better," Abigail tells you.

→ To go home, turn to page **84**.

→ To get closer to the battle, turn to page **86**.

"No, I'm going home," you say firmly.

"Then go," Abigail says. "But I don't know
how you're going to get there. You came in
our carriage."

She is right. You look around helplessly until
you notice your neighbors, Mr. and Mrs. Fields,
preparing to leave. They agree to give you a
ride home.

The journey home is a quiet one. Mrs. Fields
asks you a few questions about your family, but
you have little to say. You're still thinking about
the battle. Before you know it, you're at your
front door.

When you return home, you fall asleep in a chair. When you awake, it is early evening. Downstairs, you hear your mother crying.

You rush down the stairs. Your mother tells you the terrible news. The Union lost the battle. How could this have happened?

You run outside. Crying people are spilling out into the street. You hear that the Union Army has retreated and is headed back to the city. You wonder if your brother is all right.

"Those poor men will be hungry and injured," your mother says. "We should do something."

"We could make sandwiches and coffee for them," you say. "I'm sure they'll need help at the hospital too."

→To help your mother make food, turn to page **88**.

→To go to the hospital, turn to page **90**.

"Yes, let's go!" you say, climbing into the carriage. Slowly you bump along the road toward the battle. People have set up tables filled with food alongside the road. You wonder if it's for the soldiers or for themselves, but you don't stop to ask.

As you move closer to the battlefield, cannon fire shakes the ground like small earthquakes. The loud pop of rifles and the shouts and cries of soldiers fill the air. Men on both sides fall to the ground like rag dolls. You pray that your brother, Samuel, isn't one of them.

You stay and watch until late afternoon. It seems as if the Union is winning. You and the others cheer the soldiers as they move about the battlefield. Then, more Confederate soldiers seem to appear out of nowhere. Several groups of Union soldiers fall at once. You have a bad feeling.

Early in the battle, the Union soldiers appeared to be winning.

"Let's move farther back," you urge. "Something's not right."

"Oh, don't be such a spoilsport," Abigail says impatiently as she claps for the Union soldiers. "We're perfectly safe."

➤If you move back, turn to page **94**.

➤If you stay, turn to page **98**.

You and your mother stay up most of the night making piles of sandwiches and pots of strong, hot coffee. It begins to rain.

Late the next morning, soldiers begin to stumble into town. You're shocked at their appearance. They're soaked from the rain and filthy with sweat, dirt, soot, and blood. Most of them have dazed, empty expressions.

You and Mother hand out sandwiches and coffee. The men gratefully accept them. You frantically search the crowds for your brother, Samuel, but you don't see him.

You walk through the crowd until you run out of food. Tired and grief-stricken, you return home and sink down on the porch. You watch soldiers curl up on lawns, in the street, and in doorways to sleep.

You think of your brother. Is he trying to make his way back home? Or is he lying wounded somewhere? You won't let yourself think of the possibility that he may be dead. Wherever he is, you know that he'll soon face another battle.

"This is not a one-day war," you say to yourself. "This war will last a very long time."

THE END

To follow another path, turn to page 15.
To read the conclusion, turn to page 103.

You collect as much food, water, and clean bandages as you can carry and head downtown. You're not the only one who wants to help. A crowd of women is headed in the same direction that you are.

Soon you arrive at the Patent Office, where doctors have set up a makeshift hospital. You're stunned at the terrible wounds you see. Your stomach heaves at the awful sights and smells, but you swallow hard. You're determined to do whatever you can for these brave soldiers.

Soon a short woman strides up to you. "Are you here to help?" she demands.

"I want to do whatever I can," you reply. "Who are you?"

"I'm Clara Barton," the woman replies. "Come with me."

During the war, Clara Barton brought medical supplies to injured soldiers on battlefields.

Turn the page.

Military hospitals were built for injured soldiers later in the war.

You follow Clara to a huge pile of boxes. They're filled with combs, bandages, and other items.

"I've collected these for the men," she explains. "Hospitals don't have even the most basic supplies."

You and Clara spend several hours passing out the supplies to the injured soldiers. Finally, you are so tired that you sink into a corner. Clara finds you and pats your hand.

"You've done good work today," she says. "You have the makings of a fine nurse."

You sigh as you gaze sadly at the hundreds of soldiers now filling every space on the floor. You're afraid that there will be much more death and destruction to come.

THE END

To follow another path, turn to page 15.
To read the conclusion, turn to page 103.

"I don't like this," you say. "I'm going home."

"Suit yourself," Abigail says. "But you'll have to walk."

You begin to walk back the way you came. Soon the sounds of battle are behind you, but you still feel a sense of panic. Suddenly the road is filled with Union soldiers, all running toward Washington, D.C.

"We're done," one yells.

"Run for your lives," another says.

Soldiers push and shove, making you stumble forward. Panic fills the air. Your full hoop skirt makes it hard to get out of their way. You hear the sound of galloping horses behind you. A wagon full of wounded soldiers rushes past. You're shocked to see your brother, Samuel, hanging over the side of the wagon.

It was hard for women to move quickly in the full hoop skirts of the 1860s.

Turn the page.

"Stop!" you call. The wagon slows down enough for you to climb aboard.

"Sister, I'm so glad you're here," Samuel whispers. As you cradle Samuel's head in your lap, you see a deep wound in his shoulder. Swallowing hard, you pray that he'll get to Washington in time.

The ride is bumpy and miserable. Flies buzz around the men's open wounds. You do your best to swat them away. Several men die along the way, but Samuel is still alive. When you get to town, you ask the driver to take you home. The carriage pulls up in front of your house.

"Help!" you scream, and your parents appear at the door. Your mother sobs as you help your father carry Samuel into the house. You clean Samuel's wounds and make him comfortable.

Samuel's wounds are serious. He was shot in the shoulder and in the leg. But the bullets went cleanly through his flesh. As the night wears on, you're relieved to see that there is no sign of infection.

You and your mother tend to Samuel all night. By dawn, it appears he will live. You're happy for Samuel, but sad for all the soldiers who died that day. You know this battle is just the beginning of the long, bloody war to come.

THE END

To follow another path, turn to page 15.
To read the conclusion, turn to page 103.

You're sure that the Union forces will turn the battle around, so you decide to stay. Soon, however, it's clear that the Confederates are winning. You hear that General McDowell has ordered a retreat. The road begins to fill with rows of soldiers marching back to Washington.

You, Abigail, and John join the mob of carriages, wagons, and soldiers crowding the narrow road. Gunfire echoes behind you.

"They're after us!" a soldier yells.

The crowd panics. People rush madly away from the battlefield. You and your friends are caught up in the confusion. Abigail tries to urge the frightened horses forward, but they stop in their tracks.

Without warning, a group of soldiers overtakes your carriage. "What are you doing?" you cry.

"These men are hurt. They can't walk any longer," their leader says. Another soldier roughly hauls you out of your seat and throws you onto the dusty road. Abigail and John fall beside you. The soldiers jump into your carriage and disappear into the crowd.

Nearby, you see Senator Wilson riding bareback on a horse. As he struggles to stay on, he yells, "The Confederates shot at my wagon and tried to kill me!"

You can't believe that the Union soldiers left you to be trampled by the mob. You see tables full of food overturned by the side of the road. Hungry, dirty soldiers are grabbing everything they can. The gunfire from behind you pushes you onward with the crowds.

Turn the page.

Senator Henry Wilson was an onlooker at the battle. Later, he served as U.S. vice president.

Late the next morning, you and your friends finally reach the outskirts of Washington. Your feet are throbbing from the long walk. You're shocked at the sight that greets you. Hundreds of wounded, dirty soldiers fill the streets. You turn toward home, tired and filled with sadness. You realize that this war is going to last a long time.

THE END

To follow another path, turn to page 15.
To read the conclusion, turn to page 103.

Inexperienced soldiers caused confusion during the Battle of Bull Run.

CHAPTER 5

THE FIRST BATTLE

The Battle of Bull Run was disorganized.
Some of the soldiers were trained members
of the army. But many on both sides were
civilian volunteers. These men had only a short
time to learn how to fight before the battle.
Their inexperience caused much confusion on
the battlefield.

Uniforms were another cause of confusion.
At later battles, Confederate soldiers wore gray
uniforms. Union soldiers wore blue. At Bull
Run, though, soldiers didn't have matching
uniforms. Sometimes they didn't know if they
were facing enemy soldiers or members of
their own army.

Misinformation also played a part in the battle. When Confederate forces were driven back to Henry Hill, Union General McDowell thought his army had won. Some Confederate soldiers heard this news and started retreating.

Late in the day, Confederate reinforcements arrived. The reinforcements didn't outnumber the Union forces. But many Union soldiers saw the fresh Confederates and thought their army was beaten. Union troops began to retreat.

At first, the retreat was calm. But soon rumors that the Confederates were chasing them spread through the Union soldiers. The retreat became a riot. But by that time, the Confederates were too disorganized to chase the Union troops. About 2,000 Union soldiers and 1,700 Confederate soldiers died in the battle.

Lee surrendered to Grant in the village of Appomattox Court House, Virginia.

Bull Run was the first major battle of a bloody four-year war. The Civil War claimed the lives of about 620,000 people. It is the deadliest war in U.S. history.

The Confederates won Bull Run and several other early battles. But by 1863, the Union was winning. On April 9, 1865, Confederate General Robert E. Lee surrendered to Union General Ulysses S. Grant. The war was over at last.

The Civil War changed the United States in many ways. Slavery became illegal. Thousands of African Americans suddenly found themselves without homes, jobs, or money. Some moved to large Northern cities. Others became pioneers and headed west. Most stayed in the South and lived in conditions that weren't much better than when they were slaves.

The war destroyed many parts of the South, including the cities of Atlanta, Georgia, and Richmond, Virginia. Rebuilding was slow and difficult. Some areas never fully recovered.

The war also settled the question of whether states had a right to secede. Before the war, state governments believed they had the right to do whatever they pleased.

Much of Richmond, Virginia, was destroyed at the end of the war.

The war united the states in a way that had not been possible before. It was clear that no state had the right to leave the Union. The Civil War gave the country a sense of unity and purpose.

TIME LINE

November 1860 — Abraham Lincoln is elected president of the United States.

December 20, 1860 — South Carolina is the first Southern state to secede from the Union.

January–June 1861 — Mississippi, Florida, Alabama, Georgia, Louisiana, Texas, Virginia, Arkansas, North Carolina, and Tennessee secede. They, along with South Carolina, form the Confederacy.

April 12, 1861 — Confederates fire the first shots of the Civil War when they attack Fort Sumter.

July 16 — Union General Irvin McDowell's army marches toward Manassas Junction. The Confederate Army of the Potomac, under the command of General Pierre Beauregard, is already there.

July 18 —Union and Confederate soldiers fight a small skirmish at Blackburn's Ford.

July 21

2:30 a.m. — More Confederate soldiers arrive by train at Manassas Junction; McDowell's army begins the march toward Beauregard's Confederate forces.

5:30 a.m. — Union forces arrive at the stone bridge and take up positions.

6:00 a.m. — The battle begins.

8:30 a.m. — Confederate forces are ordered to Matthews Hill to block the Union Army.

10:30 a.m. — Several Union and Confederate brigades fight fiercely on Matthews Hill.

11:30 a.m. — After heavy fighting, the Confederates are forced to retreat from Matthews Hill. The Confederates seem to be losing the battle.

12:00 p.m. — Confederate units rush to attack the Union troops at Henry Hill.

1:00 p.m. — Several Union brigades retreat from Henry Hill.

2:30 p.m. — The Confederates capture Union cannons on Henry Hill. More Union forces retreat.

4:00 p.m. — Union brigades try to attack Henry Hill, but are defeated.

6:00 p.m. — The Union Army retreats. The Confederates win the battle.

April 9, 1865 — After four years of war, Confederate General Robert E. Lee surrenders at Appomattox Court House, Virginia.

OTHER PATHS TO EXPLORE

In this book, you've seen how the events of the Battle of Bull Run look different from three points of view.

Perspectives on history are as varied as the people who lived it. You can explore other paths on your own to learn more about what happened. Seeing history from many points of view is an important part of understanding it.

Here are some ideas for other Battle of Bull Run points of view to explore:

- ◆ Several families lived near the site of the battle. What was that experience like?

- ◆ Many people had family members or friends who fought on or supported the opposite side. How do you think these relationships affected people's actions during the war?

- ◆ If the Confederacy had won the war, what do you think life for people in this country would have been like?

THE CIVIL WAR:

AN INTERACTIVE HISTORY ADVENTURE

BY MATT DOEDEN

CONSULTANT:

MARK SNELL, PHD

PROFESSOR OF HISTORY/DIRECTOR

GEORGE TYLER MOORE CENTER FOR THE STUDY OF THE CIVIL WAR

SHEPHERD UNIVERSITY

TABLE OF CONTENTS

About Your Adventure

YOU are living in the United States in 1863. A civil war between the North and the South has divided the nation. Which side will you support? What decisions will you have to make?

In this book, you'll explore how the choices people made meant the difference between life and death. The events you'll experience happened to real people.

Chapter One sets the scene. Then you choose which path to read. Follow the directions at the bottom of each page. The choices you make will change your outcome. After you finish one path, go back and read the others for new perspectives and more adventures.

YOU CHOOSE the path
you take through history.

Confederate soldiers bombarded Fort Sumter from Fort Moultrie on April 12, 1861.

A NATION DIVIDED

The year is 1863. The United States and
the Confederate States of America are in the
middle of a bitter civil war. The war started April
12, 1861, when Confederate soldiers fired on
Fort Sumter in South Carolina. Since then, the
Yankee troops of the North and the Rebels of
the South have fought many battles.

The issues behind the war are complicated.
But you understand a few things. The South
wants its independence from the North. The
11 states of the Confederacy have seceded, or
withdrawn, from the United States. They want
their freedom from what they see as a controlling
federal government.

Turn the page.

Slavery is a central issue. Slavery is illegal in the North. Southern states want to keep the right to own slaves. On January 1, 1863, President Abraham Lincoln signed the Emancipation Proclamation. This order freed slaves living in Confederate-held areas. The North's main goal is to keep the Union together, but it also supports ending slavery in the entire country.

In the East, the Confederate army has dominated the first two years of the war. Under the leadership of Generals Robert E. Lee, Joseph Johnston, Thomas "Stonewall" Jackson, James Longstreet, and others, the Confederacy has won battle after battle. President Abraham Lincoln knows the Union needs a big victory. But he struggles to find a leader who can match up to the Confederate commander, Lee.

In the South, slaves were held in slave pens like this one before they were sold.

The situation is a little brighter for the Union in the West. Early battles focused on control of Tennessee, Missouri, and Kentucky. Although Missouri and Kentucky are slave states, they decided to stay in the Union. Even so, both states have troops who fight for the Confederacy.

Turn the page.

In April 1862, Confederate forces in the West suffered a major blow. At the bloody Battle of Shiloh in Tennessee, General Ulysses S. Grant led the Union to victory. During the battle, General Albert Sidney Johnson was killed. He commanded the Confederate forces in the West. Soon after, Union forces captured the important Mississippi River cities of Memphis, Tennessee, and New Orleans, Louisiana.

General Grant's next goal is complete control of the Mississippi River. In spring 1863, he moves his army toward the port city of Vicksburg, Mississippi. His action forces Confederate troops to retreat into the city.

By this time, the war seems to be at a turning point. If the Confederates continue their success in the East, the end may be near. But the Union army still outnumbers the Confederate forces. A few victories could quickly turn the tide and bring the Confederate army to its knees.

➻To join the Confederate army at Chancellorsville, turn to page **123**.

➻To join the Union army at Gettysburg, turn to page **153**.

➻To live as a civilian during the Union siege of Vicksburg, turn to page **181**.

Civil War army scouts and cavalry gathered information about the enemy's location and battle plans.

CHAPTER 2

A Confederate at Chancellorsville

It is the evening of April 30, 1863, in the Confederate army's camp near Fredericksburg, Virginia. Groups of men gather to play cards or dice, their laughter rising up over the camp.

You can't join in the fun just yet. You and your friend, Charles, are part of a scouting unit. Your job is to keep track of Union General Joseph Hooker's army.

You and Charles stand before General Thomas "Stonewall" Jackson and his aides. Jackson listens intently as you describe the land you've scouted. He's especially interested in any roads that run west just to the south of the Union line.

Turn the page.

"Hooker has at least 50,000 men camped near Chancellorsville, sir, and probably more on the way," you tell Jackson.

"Chancellorsville! Is that a town?" Jackson asks. "No, sir," Charles answers. "It's the Chancellor family's farmhouse. It's at the intersection of several roads along the Orange Turnpike, about 11 miles west of Fredericksburg."

Jackson nods slowly and dismisses you. "Get some sleep, men," he adds. "That's an order."

As the two of you walk away, you sigh with relief. Jackson is a gruff and intimidating man. Only General Robert E. Lee commands more respect from the men.

The Confederate army is confident. They've whipped the Union again and again. Now the largest armies of the Union and the Confederacy are moving closer. The outcome of the war could soon be decided.

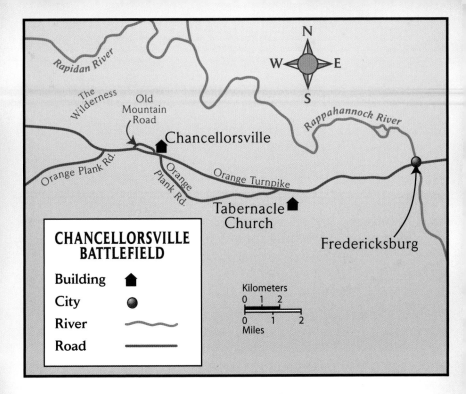

CHANCELLORSVILLE BATTLEFIELD

Building 🔼

City 🔴

River 〰️

Road ▬▬

Kilometers
0 1 2

Miles
0 1 2

"Come on," Charles says. "I know where we can get in on a poker game."

"You go ahead," you say. Tomorrow, Lee will split his forces — a huge risk. Whether you go with Stonewall Jackson to attack the Union flank or stay with the main army, you want to be rested.

→To stay with the main force, turn to page **126**.

→To march with Stonewall Jackson, turn to page **128**.

About 2:00 the next morning, May 1, Jackson marches off with about 30,000 men. They quietly move toward the Union left flank.

After Jackson's forces leave, you get a few more hours of sleep. As dawn breaks, you and Charles ride north, searching for any movement along the Yankee line.

Suddenly, you notice movement in the distance. "What was that?" you ask.

"I'm not sure," Charles replies. "Let's go look."

You ride toward a small, tree-covered ridge. You spot three people huddled behind some bushes. As you ride closer, you see their dark skin and ragged clothing. You realize that they're runaway slaves.

"You there," you say, drawing your revolver. "Come out."

Escaped slaves moved during the night and hid during the day.

A woman and two children emerge, looking terrified. "Please, sir, don't turn us in," the woman begs. "They'll whip me and punish the children."

You feel sorry for the slaves, but you are an officer in the Confederate army. Letting these people go would be a crime. You could be put in prison for helping them escape.

➤ To report the slaves, turn to page **131**.

➤ To let them go, turn to page **132**.

Long before dawn the next morning, May 1, you're back on your horse. Charles is at your side. The two of you are scouting ahead of Jackson's force of about 30,000 men. General Lee has sent him to attack the Union army near Chancellorsville. About 10,000 troops remain at the camp.

Later that morning, you reach Tabernacle Church, about 6 miles east of Chancellorsville. About 16,000 troops under the command of Confederate Generals Dick Anderson and Lafayette McLaws are digging trenches. Jackson orders these troops to join his forces. The combined forces continue marching. By nightfall, the troops are camped about 2 miles south of Chancellorsville. General Lee joins them.

Lee (center, left) and Jackson (center, right) met early the morning of May 2 to plan the attack.

Before dawn the next morning, Charles shakes you awake. "We're moving again," he says. "General Jackson's marching roundabout through the woods to stay undercover. He's planning to attack the Yankees by surprise."

By 7:30, you're back on the road. General Lee remains at the camp with Anderson and McLaws' troops. Behind you, Jackson's soldiers march in near silence.

Turn the page.

The march goes smoothly, except for an attack by Union soldiers at the rear of the column. But Hooker seems to think that the Confederate soldiers are retreating. By late afternoon, Jackson's troops are in position just outside the Union camp. They're hidden in an area of thick, tangled trees and brush called the Wilderness.

You stand by Jackson as he makes his final preparations. The men will charge at the unsuspecting Yankees from the cover of the trees. Jackson will need good officers by his side. He'll also need as many soldiers as possible to carry out the attack. Where will you serve?

➤ To join the lines, turn to page **134**.
➤ To stay by Jackson's side, turn to page **136**.

The law is the law. What happens to these people is out of your hands. "Charles, over here!" you shout. The two of you march the slaves back to a nearby farm. The owner thanks you and tells you the runaways will be punished.

When you return to camp, Lee's troops are preparing to launch several attacks. Lee hopes to keep the Union army's attention from Jackson's force. You and Charles head north with a small group. You work your way through an area of thick trees and brush called the Wilderness.

You fire a few shots at a weak point in the Union line. As the Yankees return fire, you start to retreat. You see a Union general not far ahead. You could shoot him. But you'd have to get closer, and your mission is already complete.

➤To shoot the general, turn to page **146**.
➤To return to camp, turn to page **147**.

What can you do? Turning in the slaves would be wrong, and you know it. With a deep breath, you make your decision.

"There's a large Yankee force north of here," you whisper. "Hurry. Get behind the lines to freedom."

"Thank you, sir," the woman sobs.

You hesitate and add, "If you get caught, don't tell anyone that I saw you."

"Too late for that, I'm afraid," you hear from behind you. You turn and see Charles. His pistol is drawn. It's pointed at you.

"What are you doing?" your voice cracks.

"You're helping fugitives," Charles spits. "You're betraying the Confederacy." Charles edges closer, his weapon still pointed at your chest.

"You don't have to do this," you beg.

"We'll let a court-martial decide what to do with you," Charles replies.

You don't know what to do. If you go with Charles, you might be put in prison. The slaves will be returned to their owner, where they'll suffer for their escape attempt. But the only other choice is to attack Charles and attempt to get away.

➤*To defend yourself and try to escape, turn to page* **140**.

➤*To do as you're told, turn to page* **142**.

Confederate soldiers moved quietly through the Wilderness toward the Union camp.

You take a position along the front lines, eager to be part of the charge. It's suppertime, and you can smell bacon and potatoes frying in the Yankee camp. You've had little to eat since the march began, and your mouth waters.

Finally, the order comes. You and your fellow soldiers burst out of the woods, letting out your famous Rebel yell. The Yankees are caught completely off guard. They scatter, desperately trying to form lines of defense.

A haze of smoke rolls across the battlefield as the Confederate troops advance. The sound of gunfire fills the air. Horses try to flee from the noise. The Yankees finally organize a defense, but it's too late. You scream and cheer as you help lead a charge at the main Union line.

In the distance, you see Yankee soldiers getting ready to fire a cannon into the Confederate line. The cannon is pointed in your direction!

→To charge at the cannon, turn to page **144**.

→To take cover, turn to page **148**.

Union soldiers tried to organize a defense against the surprise attack.

You stay with Jackson and his aides as he orders the attack. Together, you watch as the Confederate troops storm out of the woods. The Yankees are caught by surprise as the loud Rebel yell rings out over the field. The Union soldiers desperately try to organize themselves and form a defense. A few succeed, but most aren't able to get ready in time.

The attack is fast and furious. "Press forward!" Jackson shouts. The Yankees turn and run for their lives. They leave rifles, equipment, and dead and wounded soldiers behind them.

As the sun sets, Jackson's troops chase the Yankees until the growing darkness stops them in their tracks. Some soldiers remain along the Orange Plank Road to watch for Yankee scouts or straggling soldiers.

You figure that Jackson will be pleased with the huge victory. Instead, he seems annoyed that the Union has until morning to regroup. Despite the darkness, Jackson wants to ride forward, closer to the lines.

➤To go with Jackson, turn to page **138**.

➤To stay with the men guarding the road, turn to page **139**.

You ride on the Orange Plank Road behind the general and his aides. Jackson is eager to continue pressing the Yankee line.

You can hear Union soldiers ahead. "It's not safe for you here, General," cautions one of Jackson's aides. Reluctantly, the general agrees. You turn your horses and make your way back toward your line. As you cross Old Mountain Road, you sense movement ahead of you. But before you can call out, gunfire follows. A man to your left slumps and falls from his horse.

"Cease firing!" shouts someone in your group. "You're firing into your own men!"

You realize what has happened. The soldiers guarding the road have confused your group for Yankee cavalry. You leap from your horse.

Turn to page **150.**

You stay back as the general and his aides ride forward. You join a small group of guards who are watching the Orange Plank Road for Yankee scouts.

Trees are all around your position, making it even harder to see. After a little while, you hear muffled voices and the sound of horses approaching. Dark figures emerge ahead. Are they friends or enemies?

You're not sure what to do. If Yankees are approaching, you have to fire before they fire at you. But you're not sure who or what you'd be firing at in the darkness.

While you're thinking, one of the guards in your group fires a shot. Other guards follow his lead.

To join in the firing, turn to page **149**.

To wait to shoot, turn to page **150**.

You have just one chance. You turn to the slaves huddled in the brush and shout, "Run!" Then you lunge toward Charles, launching yourself from your horse's back. You knock the pistol from his hand.

Charles' horse rears back in surprise, throwing him to the ground. You quickly kick away his weapon and point your gun at him.

"Get down on the ground," you shout. You look back and see the woman and children running toward the north.

"You'll go to prison for this," Charles growls. "You can never return to the army. You'll be a deserter and a fugitive."

"If I kill you, nobody will ever know," you reply coldly. But even as you say the words, you know that you could never go through with it.

Charles is right. You can't go back. You have no choice but to desert the army.

You climb back onto your horse, your gun still pointed at Charles. You grab the reins of Charles' horse and lead it away. It'll take Charles hours to get back to the main army. The extra time will give you a head start.

You ride west. You know you can never go home now. You might go to Kansas or even to Texas. It will be a long, difficult ride. But you decide it's your best chance for a new life.

141

THE END

To follow another path, turn to page 121.
To read the conclusion, turn to page 211.

Your shoulders slump as you make your decision. Charles takes your weapon and marches the slaves back to a nearby farm. Then he leads you back to camp.

Charles tells General Lee what happened. Lee looks disappointed, but he says that he needs every man, including you, for the battle. He's planning several small attacks on the Union line. Lee wants to keep the enemy's attention away from Jackson's troops. Lee needs more information about the Union line, so he sends you to get a better look.

You ride carefully, staying under the cover of the Wilderness. Smoke in the distance tells you that you're getting close to the Union army.

Suddenly, you hear a snap from behind you. You spin around. Three Union soldiers stand with their guns pointed at you.

The Union captured about 462,000 Confederate soldiers during the war.

"Get down," one of them orders. You throw down your weapon and climb off your horse. The men march you into the Union camp. You'll be questioned and sent to a Union prison. If the Confederacy is going to win the war, it will have to do it without you.

THE END

To follow another path, turn to page 121.
To read the conclusion, turn to page 211.

Wounded soldiers awaited treatment near the battlefields.

With your sharp bayonet fixed to the front of your rifle, you charge at the Yankee troops who are firing the cannon. They see you coming, but it's too late. You crash into one soldier, the blade of your bayonet plunging deep into his stomach.

Another Yankee raises a pistol at you. You smash the butt of your rifle into his face, and he slumps to the ground. By this time, your fellow soldiers have noticed what's happening. Charles and another soldier race over, firing. A third Yankee falls to the ground.

As you turn to rejoin the battle, you hear a small click. Too late, you realize what it is. The man you stuck with the bayonet is clutching a pistol. You dive for cover just as he takes the shot. It catches you in the left shoulder. You cry out in pain as Charles shoots and kills the Yankee. You try to stand, but Charles stops you.

"Stay there," he says. "The Yankees are falling back. We'll get you help."

You lay there as the battle rages on. Your wound is painful, but you don't think your life is in danger. The battle will likely be a victory for your side, and you're proud of the role you played.

THE END

To follow another path, turn to page 121.
To read the conclusion, turn to page 211.

This could be a big opportunity. As the other men begin to fall back, you dash forward. Soon the general is within range. But the Yankees have spotted you as well. You dive to the ground and prepare to shoot. But Union troops quickly surround the general and raise their rifles.

Several shots whiz over your head, barely missing. You turn to run, but as you stand, you feel a sharp stinging in your left leg. The leg gives out, and you crash back down to the ground.

Seeing you down, several Union soldiers charge. You turn and raise your weapon. Bam! You're hit again, this time in the chest. Your weapon falls from your grasp as blackness closes in around your eyes. You've given your life for the Confederacy.

THE END

To follow another path, turn to page 121.
To read the conclusion, turn to page 211.

You've completed your mission. There's no need to risk your life. The important thing is that Jackson's forces succeed against the Union flank.

"Fall back!" you shout. The small group of soldiers makes its way back to the camp. That evening, you learn that Lee and Jackson's plan worked. The Confederacy won the day's battle. But there isn't much celebrating in the camp. Word comes that Jackson has been shot.

The battle continues for the next three days. Finally, on May 6, General Hooker retreats for the last time. On May 10, Jackson dies. You helped win a major battle, but the price was huge. You hope the Confederacy can still win the war without one of its finest generals.

THE END

To follow another path, turn to page 121.
To read the conclusion, turn to page 211.

"Get down!" you shout. You dive to the ground, holding your hands over your head.

When you look up, you realize you're the only one on the ground. Two other Confederate soldiers are charging the Yankee cannon. You feel ashamed. You leap to your feet to join the charge.

You raise your rifle and start to run toward the cannon. You hear what sounds like a boom of thunder. In an instant, you're thrown to the ground. Pain surges through your body. When you look down, your right leg is gone.

You hear the groans of several men nearby. You feel very cold. And you can't really feel the pain anymore. As your eyes slowly close, you know you won't be waking up again.

THE END

To follow another path, turn to page 121.
To read the conclusion, turn to page 211.

General Stonewall Jackson was shot accidentally by his fellow troops.

You raise your rifle and join in the fire. Several men in the other group fall to the ground.

"Cease firing! You're firing into your own men!" you hear. "General Jackson is hit in three places," someone else shouts.

You stand there in a daze while others rush to help the fallen general. What if your bullet was one of the shots that hit Jackson?

Turn to page 151.

After the shooting stops, you see several men gathered around a figure lying on the ground. With horror, you realize that it's General Jackson. He's been hit once in his right hand and twice in his left arm.

"Get a stretcher!" you shout. "The general is hit!"

You turn to Jackson. "Are you hurt badly, sir?" you ask.

"I fear my arm is broken," he replies.

A doctor and one of Jackson's aides bandage his wounds. You feel helpless as Jackson is loaded onto a stretcher and carried away. Now all you can do is pray that Jackson will be all right.

The battle continues for three more days. On May 6, Hooker's army retreats across the Rappahannock River. The Confederates have scored a major victory.

At first, doctors believe General Jackson will recover. But he develops pneumonia and dies on May 10. His death is a terrible blow to the Confederacy.

You and Charles see General Lee later that day. He's always been strong and confident, but you can tell Jackson's death has shaken him badly. "Let's go," Charles says as you watch Lee ride away. "This war won't end for one man."

The two of you ride off. You know you'll keep fighting to honor your country and preserve your way of life.

THE END

To follow another path, turn to page 121.
To read the conclusion, turn to page 211.

Colonel Joshua Chamberlain (front) led the 20th Maine Infantry into battle.

THREE DAYS IN GETTYSBURG

It is July 1, 1863. Night has fallen over the countryside. You've been marching for days in the Maryland and Pennsylvania heat, so you're grateful for the cooler night air. Your tattered Union army uniform is soaked in sweat and covered in dirt.

You're a private serving under Colonel Joshua Chamberlain in the Union Army of the Potomac. Your regiment, the 20th Maine Infantry, is marching to a little town called Gettysburg, Pennsylvania. There, the main armies of the Union and the Confederacy have met to battle. The fighting began early this morning.

Turn the page.

As your regiment comes around a bend in the road, you're ordered to stop. You are several miles from Gettysburg. You see a few large wooded ridges and hills that dot the flat landscape.

"That's it?" asks George, your closest friend. "Seems like a strange place to fight a battle that may decide the war." You nod, too tired to talk.

You've heard this will be a big battle. General George Meade, the new Union commander, will make his stand against Confederate General Robert E. Lee. Failure to drive back the Rebels could leave the U.S. capital, Washington, D.C., at risk of being captured.

The next afternoon, July 2, the heavy fighting begins. Your regiment is placed at the far end of the Union line. You're defending a wooded hill called Little Round Top. You and the other soldiers take cover behind boulders and trees.

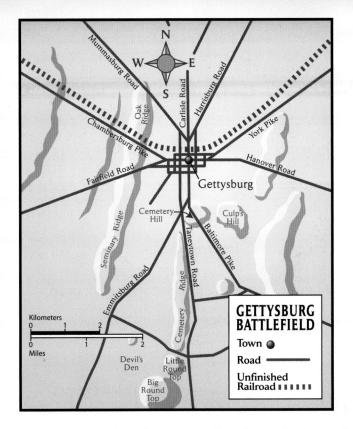

Colonel Chamberlain walks along the line of troops. He looks over the men as he strokes his long mustache. "The Rebels will attack the hill soon," he says. "The high ground will give us the advantage. We cannot fall back. If we fail, the Rebels will circle around behind and attack our lines from both sides. This is it, men."

Turn the page.

Soon, you hear a high-pitched wailing called the Rebel yell. The Confederates are attacking. An officer runs toward you. "I need reinforcement on the left flank," he shouts at you, George, and several nearby soldiers. The officer points to a spot about 50 feet down the line.

"I'll go, sir," George replies.

"George!" you say once the officer is out of earshot. "You're putting yourself right in the line of fire."

George shrugs and slings his rifle over his shoulder. "I came here to fight. You coming with me or not?"

→To stay where you are, go to page 157.

→To join George on the flank, turn to page 158.

"Good luck," you tell George, shaking his hand. "I'm going to take my chances here."

You watch George take his position as you take cover behind a boulder. You can't see very far. The shouts of the advancing Rebels are getting louder. The sound of gunshots is deafening.

Before you know it, the first attack is upon you. You take careful, well-aimed shots. You see a Confederate officer and fire. The officer spins and falls as your shot hits him in the shoulder.

Out of the corner of your eye, you see George. He's been hit! His right arm is bleeding, and his rifle has fallen from his grasp. He's lying right in the line of fire.

➺*To get up to help your friend, turn to page **159**.*

➺*To hold your position, turn to page **160**.*

"Okay, I'm with you," you answer. You and George walk to the end of the Union line.

As you take your place, waves of gray and brown Confederate uniforms pour out of the woods. You take aim and fire. A Rebel soldier falls to the ground, screaming. While you reload, several Confederates charge at you and George. As they take aim, you pull George to the ground. An enemy shot whizzes overhead, right where you had just been standing.

From your knees, you take aim again. You see a Confederate soldier out in the open. But he's on the ground, holding his leg. Farther back, you see a Rebel officer urging his men on in the attack. It will be a tough shot to hit him from such a distance, but he seems like the bigger threat.

→To take the shot at the officer, turn to page **162**.

→To take the shot at the soldier, turn to page **168**.

"George!" you shout, running. Shots whiz past as you stand up. George sees you coming and stumbles to get up. You can only watch in horror as another shot hits him square in the gut. He slumps to the ground.

"No!" you scream as you rush to his side, barely aware of the danger. Another shot whistles by, so close that you can almost feel it.

George is pale and cool by the time you reach him. "Tell my wife that I love her," he whispers.

"Hold on," you tell him, trying to help him up. If you can get George to the rear of the line, he might make it. But he's fighting you.

"No," he coughs. "Get yourself back to cover." You know that he's right. You'll be safer if you stay low. But unless you can move him, George will die — and soon.

➤ To get back behind cover, turn to page **160**.

➤ To move George to safety, turn to page **179**.

You feel helpless, knowing there's nothing you can do for your friend. But helping him now would be almost certain death. You duck behind a boulder.

A nearby shot quickly focuses your attention back to the attacking Confederates. You slowly raise your rifle and squeeze off a single shot. A Confederate soldier drops to the ground.

The battle rages on. Smoke rolls across the battlefield. Eventually, the Confederates retreat. Taking deep, heavy breaths, you wipe the sweat from your face. You can't see George anymore, but you know he must be dead. There's no time to mourn your friend, though. Before long, the Confederates will be back.

The Confederates charge again, fighting bravely. But you and your regiment have the high ground. Once again, you force them to retreat.

Soldiers on Little Round Top took shelter behind large boulders.

"Save your ammunition, men!" shouts the colonel. You check your supply. You started with 60 rounds. There are only six shots left.

The man to your right looks at you. You recognize him as John, your neighbor from back home. "I'm out," he says. "Quick, give me some of your ammunition before they come again."

➤To give John the ammunition, turn to page **164**.

➤To keep your ammunition, turn to page **170**.

The 20th Maine used bayonets to force the Confederates to retreat.

You take aim at the officer and gently squeeze the trigger. The officer jumps as the shot whizzes by. You missed, but it doesn't matter. Within moments, the Rebels are retreating. You and George join in the cheering as the regiment celebrates the victory. "We did it!" you shout.

"No, that was just the first attack. They'll be back," George answers.

Sure enough, the Rebels attack again and again. Soon, you're out of ammunition. So is George and most of the regiment.

"Bayonet!" shouts Colonel Chamberlain. You take the long, sharp blade and secure it to the front of your rifle.

The regiment stands and rushes down to meet the Confederates. They're surprised by the move, giving the Union soldiers an advantage. Before you have a chance to get in on the action, the Rebels are in full retreat. This time, with sunset quickly approaching, there's real cause for celebration. You've held the line.

Not far from you, a Confederate soldier is stumbling away in retreat. He's limping badly, and you know you could catch him. You run at the fleeing soldier. He sees you coming and raises a rifle in your direction.

➻*To try to take the soldier prisoner, turn to page 166.*

➻*To let him go, turn to page 167.*

"Here. Don't waste them," you say as you hand three precious cartridges to John. You have just enough time to get a drink of water before the battle is on again. The Rebels are coming closer than ever, determined to break through the line.

The attack is shockingly swift. You fire a shot and then another. The Rebels keep coming closer and closer. An enemy shot hits the boulder in front of you. "Get down," shouts John. You duck, and he fires a shot over your head. It hits an enemy soldier who had been aiming right at you.

"Now, aren't you glad you gave me some ammunition?" John asks you.

Together, you reload and fire one last shot. Your ammunition is gone, and you're not the only one. The regiment has all but run out. How will you stop the Rebel advance?

"Bayonet!" shouts Colonel Chamberlain. You take the long, sharp blade and secure it to the front of your rifle.

You move away from the safety of the boulder and rush downhill with your regiment. The counterattack surprises the Rebel troops. In moments, you're in the thick of the battle. Out of the corner of your eye, you spot a Confederate officer in front of you. He's aiming a pistol right at Colonel Chamberlain.

→*To try to kill the officer with your bayonet, turn to page **172**.*

→*To try to tackle him instead, turn to page **173**.*

"He's bluffing," you think, hoping he's out of ammunition as well. You take a few more steps and watch as he slowly lowers his rifle. You were right. You raise your bayonet and shout for the soldier to surrender. He holds up his empty hands and allows you to take him.

"Come with me," you say gruffly.

You march the man back behind the Union line, turning him over to a sergeant. Maybe the man will have information about the Rebel plans. And if not, at least he won't be able to attack again. He'll be sent to a prison camp to wait out the rest of the war.

"Good work, private," Colonel Chamberlain tells you, putting his hand on your shoulder. "You should feel proud of what you've done today."

Turn to page 177.

The battlefield of Gettysburg was crowded and filled with confusion.

You and the Confederate soldier stare at each other for several moments. You can see in his eyes that he is as tired as you are. He looks like a young man, but there are already gray streaks in his full beard.

Both of you lower your weapons at the same time. Without taking his eyes off you, the Confederate takes a careful step backward. You do the same, nodding. The man turns and runs down the hill. You turn and rejoin your regiment. The fighting is over, at least for today.

Turn to page 177.

You take aim at the wounded Rebel soldier and squeeze the trigger. The man is thrown backward as the shot slams into his chest. Meanwhile, George takes a shot at the officer. He misses, and the Rebels keep coming.

As you reload, George shouts, "Get down!" As you turn to look, you feel a strange sensation in your stomach. You drop your rifle and run your hand along the front of your uniform. It's slick with blood.

George fires a shot, then ducks down. "A gut shot. Hold on," he says over the gunfire. He grabs your loaded rifle and fires it.

"They're falling back!" he tells you. You can hear the whooping and shouting of your regiment. George shouts for help. As you begin to lose consciousness, other soldiers carry you off the field.

Doctors and nurses set up field hospitals in tents near battlefields.

You wake up in a field hospital. You overhear the low voice of a doctor nearby. "There's nothing I can do for him," he says. You know he's talking about you.

For three days, you drift in and out of consciousness. A shot to the stomach is one of the slowest and most painful ways to die. When death finally comes, you welcome it.

THE END

To follow another path, turn to page 121.
To read the conclusion, turn to page 211.

"Find someone else," you answer. "I don't have enough."

John scowls and moves down the line, asking for ammunition. A short time later, the Rebels charge again. The attack is even more furious than the earlier charges. Gray and brown uniforms are everywhere. As you fire a shot into the madness, splinters of wood from a nearby tree shatter into the air.

Moments later, a bullet catches you in the left arm. The force of it throws you back several feet. Your head cracks against a boulder, and you lose consciousness.

The next thing you remember, you're lying in a crowded field hospital. The sounds of wounded and dying men fill the air. Weakly, you call for help. You feel a hand on your shoulder as a doctor looks at your wound.

"Sorry, son, but this arm will have to go," the doctor tells you. He puts a cloth over your mouth and tells you to inhale. The fumes cause you to drift out of consciousness. You know that when you awake, your left arm will be gone.

You've survived the bloodiest battle of the war, but you've paid a heavy price. The stump at the end of your left shoulder will always remind you of your part in the battle of Gettysburg.

171

THE END

To follow another path, turn to page 121.
To read the conclusion, turn to page 211.

In a rage, you run at the Confederate officer. Just as he's about to shoot, you thrust your bayonet into his belly. Surprised, he turns. His dark brown eyes stare into yours. He stumbles, raises the pistol, and fires.

At first, you're not sure what's happened. Then you feel it. You've been shot in the chest. Air rushes from your lungs as you lift your hand to the wound. Together, you and the officer fall to the ground, eyes still locked.

"It's a good death," he whispers. The darkness is creeping in all around you. All you can do is nod.

You die on the field of Gettysburg, your head resting on the body of the Confederate you killed. Your last thought is, "Was it all worth it?"

THE END

To follow another path, turn to page 121.
To read the conclusion, turn to page 211.

You shout as you slam into the officer. He sprawls to the ground, his pistol flying out of his grasp. He quickly gets up, turns around, and runs away. His fellow Confederates soon follow. You've done it! You've beaten back the Rebel charge once again.

The field is littered with bodies and blood. In the confusing aftermath, you find George's body and say a prayer.

As night closes in, you and your fellow soldiers fall into an exhausted sleep. You wake with a start when you hear Colonel Chamberlain's voice. "Boys, we've been asked to occupy that hill in front," he says, pointing in the darkness in the direction of Big Round Top. "Do I have some volunteers?"

Turn the page.

Union troops retreated to Cemetery Hill on July 1. The hill was also the site of heavy fighting on July 2 and 3.

You try to shake off the sleep as you rise to your feet. Looking around, you see all the other soldiers on their feet too. With only the full moon as a guide, you make your way quietly up Big Round Top. You spend the night half-asleep behind a boulder, waiting for the sun to rise.

Early the next morning, July 3, you and the other soldiers build a stone wall for protection. About 1:00 in the afternoon, you hear a loud thundering noise. The battle is in full swing again, about a mile north of your regiment's protected position.

After two hours, the shelling ends. The silence is eerie. You slowly move away from the stone wall as the news spreads.

You learn Lee attacked the heart of the Union line at a place called Cemetery Ridge. Major General George Pickett and his Virginia soldiers led about 12,000 Confederate troops across an open field separating the lines. It was a last, desperate charge. The Union soldiers were ready for them, with plenty of reinforcements. By late afternoon, more than half of the Confederate soldiers are dead, wounded, or captured.

Turn the page.

The battle is an important but costly Union victory. You hear that about 23,000 Union soldiers are dead, injured, or missing. The Confederate losses were even greater, with about 28,000 dead, injured, or missing soldiers.

You think about George and the other brave men who died on both sides. You wonder if there were really any winners in this bloody battle.

THE END

To follow another path, turn to page 121.
To read the conclusion, turn to page 211.

Confederate General Lewis Armistead (top, right) led his brigade during Pickett's Charge.

The Union forces regroup as night falls. Your regiment is reassigned to defend Big Round Top. You spend the night huddled against a boulder on the hill. Early the next morning, your regiment builds a stone wall for protection. You stay behind the wall most of the day. The heavy fighting is about a mile to your north.

That afternoon, Lee orders a charge at the very heart of the Union line, at a place called Cemetery Ridge. It's a last, desperate attack.

Turn the page.

The Union army is ready. Cannons boom as the brave Confederate soldiers try to cross an open field. The attack is doomed, and soon the Confederates are driven back.

"I can't believe they charged," George says when it's over. "General Lee should have fallen back and regrouped."

"Is the war over?" you ask. "Can the Rebels recover from this defeat?

"It's far from over," George answers. "We hurt them badly here. But they'll keep fighting."

"So will we," you say. You look down at the smoldering battlefield. The bodies of soldiers from both sides are scattered everywhere. It's a Union victory, but a costly one. The war will go on. You just hope you live to see the end of it.

THE END

To follow another path, turn to page 121.
To read the conclusion, turn to page 211.

"Never," you tell your friend. "I'm not giving up on you." But even as you say the words, you see your friend's face growing paler.

You hook your arm under George's shoulder and around his back. He moans weakly as you lift him from the ground. The sounds of gunfire fill the air. You hear something whiz past your ear.

Suddenly, you feel a strange tingling in your side. The strength in your legs gives out. You've been hit! The two of you collapse to the ground as the fight rages on. Instantly, you know it's bad. When you put your hand to your side, it's stained bright red with blood.

"Sorry, friend," George whispers to you, just before his eyes close one last time. You're sad you won't live to see the end of the battle. But at least you'll die with your best friend at your side.

THE END

To follow another path, turn to page 121.
To read the conclusion, turn to page 211.

Union gunboats shelled
Vicksburg from the Mississippi
River during the siege.

CHAPTER 4

LIVING UNDER SIEGE

A low, rumbling sound fills the air. It sounds like thunder, but you know that it's really Union cannons. They boom night and day, shelling your beloved city of Vicksburg, Mississippi.

You hold tightly to the hand of your sister, Anna. She's only 12 years old — six years younger than you. With your mother dead and your father serving in the Confederate army, you're all the family she has. You have almost become used to the shelling over the past weeks, but that doesn't make it any less terrifying. You miss your husband, who is off serving with the Confederate army. You'd been married only a few weeks before he had to leave for war.

Turn the page.

You never thought it would come to this. In May, Confederate soldiers fought off two Union attacks. Then, Union General Ulysses S. Grant ordered a siege of Vicksburg. He's blocking supplies from entering the city and trying to blast it into surrender. With its location on the Mississippi River, Vicksburg is important to the Confederate defense. If the city falls, the Union will take a big step toward choking off an already undersupplied Confederate army. General John Pemberton commands the 20,000 soldiers who defend the city from the much larger Union force.

The shelling is getting closer. A house not far from your own was hit last night.

"It's getting too dangerous to stay here, even if we hide in the cellar," Anna reminds you. "Almost all of the other women and children have fled to the caves."

Union soldiers also took shelter in dugouts on Vicksburg's hillsides.

You know that she's right. Few people have died during the shelling, but thousands have taken shelter in caves dug in the hills near the city. But you don't want to leave your home. The thought of living in the cold, damp caves seems almost too terrible to bear.

→To stay in your home, turn to page **184**.

→To take shelter in the caves, turn to page **189**.

"We're not leaving our home," you tell Anna. "There isn't a safe place in this city right now. At least here, we've got a little food and comfortable beds."

The Union navy joins the army in shelling the city. You stay in the cellar that night. The booming of cannon fire makes sleep impossible. But at least you're at home.

Just before dawn, you hear a scratching sound from above. Carefully, you climb the cellar stairs. You hear voices from inside the pantry. Thieves! They're stealing what little food you've got!

The thieves don't know that you're there. Who knows what they might do if you call out. Do they have guns? Are they so hungry that they'd kill for a few bags of flour? But if you do nothing, what will you and Anna eat?

You decide that confronting the thieves is too dangerous. Maybe someone outside could help. Or maybe you should sneak back down into the cellar and wait for them to leave. You can deal with hunger. You can't deal with facing a shotgun or pistol.

→ *To sneak back down to the cellar, turn to page* **186**.

→ *To run into the street and call for help, turn to page* **187**.

As quietly as you can, you sneak back into the cellar and lock yourself inside. You know that all of your food will be gone, but at least you and Anna will be safe. After a few minutes, the sounds from upstairs stop. The thieves have left, but you're not about to go back up there until the sun is up.

In the morning, your fears are confirmed. The thieves took almost all of your food. Strangely, they didn't bother taking any valuables. You were sure at least your silverware would be gone.

When Anna gets up, you break the bad news. "I hate to do it, but it's just not safe here," you tell her. "We have no choice left but to go to the caves."

Turn to page 189.

You dash outside into the street.

"Help!" you cry. "I'm being robbed!"

Your voice echoes up and down the street. There's not a soul to be seen. Most of your neighbors have moved to the caves.

From inside, you hear scrambling noises. The thieves have heard you. What if they're coming outside to get you? You dart to the side of the house and hide behind some shrubs. You hear the house's back door slam shut. "Let's get out of here," whispers a man. "General Pemberton will have our heads if he finds out about this."

You realize with horror that the thieves are Confederate soldiers! The thought gives you a chill. The very men who are supposed to be protecting you are now stealing from you.

Turn the page.

The sound of hurried footsteps slowly fades away. You wait in your hiding spot for several minutes before going back inside. You tiptoe into the house and light a lamp. One look in the pantry shows you that the thieves made off with almost all of your food.

You're furious. The thieves had mentioned General John Pemberton, the commander of the Confederate army defending Vicksburg. Should you report the incident to the Confederate officers? Or would it be just a waste of time?

➤To go to General Pemberton's headquarters to report the theft, turn to page **195**.

➤To drop the matter and go in search of food, turn to page **198**.

Many people often gathered in one small cave during the siege.

"Let's go," you say with a sigh.

You and Anna quickly pack a few things. You take what little food you have. You each bring a change of clothes, blankets, and a few small valuables.

The city streets are all but deserted as you make your way to the caves. Small cooking fires burn outside the caves as you look for a spot to settle. Thin, exhausted faces watch you. Almost all of them are women, children, and the elderly.

Turn the page.

"This won't be so bad," you say hopefully, though you really don't believe it.

The caves are bustling with activity. Several slaves are cooking soup in large pots above ground. As you and Anna settle into a small dugout, you spread the blankets over the dirt floor. At least you'll have a place to sleep.

One of Anna's school friends, Edward, sees you and comes running over. "Hi, Anna!" he says excitedly. "Did you hear? General Pemberton has asked civilians to search for unexploded Yankee shells. Our soldiers need the gunpowder inside. Do you want to help me find some?"

Anna looks at you, her eyes bright with interest. You can tell she wants to go. But going out to look for shells could be dangerous.

➼*To agree to look for shells, go to page* **191**.

➼*To refuse, turn to page* **193**.

"I guess we should do our part to help the army," you say reluctantly. "But it will be dark soon. Let's go in the morning."

"Great!" says Edward. Sure enough, he's back at dawn, ready to go. The three of you make your way out into the abandoned city streets. You see a few other people searching, but nobody has found anything.

Suddenly, Edward shouts. He's found a large unexploded mortar shell. The three of you stand looking at it. "It's going to be heavy," Edward says. "Help me carry it."

"Wait," you say, hesitant. You know how powerful this weapon is. Suddenly, you don't want anything to do with it. "Maybe we should just tell a soldier where it is."

Turn the page.

The Confederate army had a large arsenal of weapons at Vicksburg.

"Don't be silly," Edward says, sighing. "This is what we came out here to do. The army needs the gunpowder. Now are you going to help me or not?"

→To help Edward pick up the shell, turn to page **200**.

→To back away, turn to page **207**.

192

You give Anna a sharp look and shake your head. "Sorry, Edward, but I think we'd rather stay where we're safe."

The boy frowns and shrugs his shoulders. "All right, then," he says, and wanders off.

"We should have helped," Anna says. "What are we going to do here? Just sit around and feel sorry for ourselves?"

You sigh. "I'm just too hungry to do anything," you answer. "Tomorrow we have to find some more food."

A woman in a nearby dugout motions for you to come over. She is thin and pale and looks very tired. With a shock, you recognize her as your mother's old friend, Clara. She appears to have aged 20 years since the spring.

Turn the page.

"I'm so glad to see you two," Clara says, giving Anna a big hug. "Come, you must be hungry. My servant is making some supper. It's not much, but you're welcome to eat with us."

"Oh, thank you," you say, finally managing a genuine smile. The thought of a hot meal sounds wonderful. A few minutes later, a young slave girl brings down a pot filled with some sort of stew. The girl fills three bowls and hands them to you, Anna, and Clara.

"What is it?" Anna asks.

"Better not to ask," Clara replies.

Anna makes a face. "It's rat, isn't it?"

"Meat is meat," Clara says, "and the two of you need the energy. Now eat up."

➻To eat the rat soup, turn to page **201**.

➻To refuse, turn to page **203**.

You take Anna by the hand and march down to the general's headquarters. A young soldier greets you, and you explain what has happened.

The soldier's face darkens. "It's certainly possible, ma'am. But I don't know what I can do if you can't identify the men."

"Will you tell the general?" you ask.

"No, the general has a lot on his mind. He doesn't need to know about every little problem."

Just then, you hear heavy footsteps. "What don't I need to know, sergeant?"

To your shock, there stands General John Pemberton himself. Northern-born, he doesn't speak with the familiar Southern accent. You explain what happened and why you think it was Confederate soldiers who robbed you.

Turn the page.

General John Pemberton commanded Confederate forces at Vicksburg.

Pemberton breathes a long, heavy sigh. "I'm sorry, ma'am. Our men only get some flour, cowpeas, and a bit of bacon each day. They're hungry. Some are getting desperate."

"So what will you do?" you ask.

Pemberton looks at the young soldier. "Have the quartermaster give these ladies a bag of flour," he orders. "I'm sorry it's not more," he adds, turning to you. "We haven't much to spare. I'd advise you to go to the caves. Your home is not a safe place to stay. Good day, ladies."

Sadly, you agree. The house just isn't safe anymore. You and Anna pack a few clothes, blankets, and valuables and make your way to the caves.

*Turn to page **209**.*

There's no point in reporting the theft. After all, you can't even identify the thieves. You and Anna take the little money you have left and head into the city. You hope to find some beef or pork, but nobody has any for sale.

"I have mule meat and dog meat for sale," cracks the voice of an old man across the street. "Interested?" His eyes gleam greedily.

"How much for the mule?" you ask.

"Five dollars," he replies.

"Five dollars?" you gasp. "We can't afford that."

"Two dollars for the dog, then." Anna looks at you with horror. "We can't eat dog," she insists.

You don't have a lot of choices. You can either buy the dog meat or trap rats for food. Neither idea is very appealing.

→ To refuse the man's offer, go to page **199**.

→ To buy the dog meat, turn to page **205**.

"No thank you, sir. Good day," you answer. You take Anna by the hand and stomp away.

The two of you make it back home before you break down in tears. "What are we going to do?" you ask.

"I'd rather eat rats than dog," Anna says.

You nod slowly. "Come on, let's go inside," you say. But just as you stand up, a shell crashes into the house next door. Wood splinters and glass shatters. You both throw yourselves to the ground, covering your ears.

The house is destroyed. Luckily, nobody has been living there for more than a week. The family who owns it fled to the caves. You know that you have to do the same.

Quickly, you pack a few things and hurry down to the caves. You'd hoped to avoid it, but there's just no other choice.

Turn to page **209**.

Edward is right. You need to get this shell to the trenches where the Confederate defenders are dug in.

"All right," you say, slowly approaching the shell. "But Anna, you stay back. Edward and I can handle this."

Scowling, Anna steps back. You and Edward stand over the shell and work your hands beneath it. "On three," he says. "One, two . . . three!" Together, you lift the shell to waist height. Edward smiles, saying "See, that wasn't so . . ."

Boom!

The shell explodes, sending fragments of metal flying in all directions. The violent explosion kills both you and Edward before you even realize what happened.

THE END

To follow another path, turn to page 121.
To read the conclusion, turn to page 211.

With a sigh, you take the soup and lift a spoonful to your lips. In truth, there's very little meat in it. You can almost fool yourself into believing that it's chicken.

As the siege continues, you and Anna do all you can to survive. Soon, the thought of eating rat isn't even disgusting anymore. It's just the way things are. Once in awhile, if you're lucky, you get a piece of mule meat or corn bread.

Soon, clean water is almost as scarce as food. You wait in line for a single bucket. There's no water for bathing, and the caves smell of old, musty sweat.

The shelling continues. Nothing General Pemberton and the Confederate army do seems to matter. On July 3, the rumor that Pemberton will surrender swirls through the caves. You can't decide whether you're sad or relieved.

Turn the page.

The surrender formally happens on Independence Day, July 4. Soon, you and Anna return to your home, which has suffered only minor damage. Before long, life is almost back to normal.

The fall of Vicksburg is a terrible blow to the Confederate army. You hope the war will end soon. Maybe then your husband will return home and life can go on. You just pray he's still alive.

THE END

To follow another path, turn to page 121.
To read the conclusion, turn to page 211.

"Rat? You can't be serious," you say, handing the bowl back to Clara. "I'll never be hungry enough to eat vermin!"

You grab Anna's arm, causing her to spill her soup. "But I'm hungry," she cries as you drag her back to your dugout.

That night, you use a little of the flour you have left to make biscuits. The hard biscuits taste terrible and do little to fill your growling stomachs. Anna cries herself to sleep. You lie awake for hours, trying to ignore your hunger pangs.

After a few days, Anna decides to eat rat. But you never change your mind. You survive by eating any other scrap of food you can find. An old, rotten apple is like a treasure.

Turn the page.

Some civilians were hurt or killed by Union shells that missed their mark.

Soon you're too weak to leave the caves. You're lying down one day when a shell blasts into the ground above you. The cave ceiling gives way, dumping tons of rock on top of you.

Your dying thought is of Anna. You pray she'll do what you couldn't — survive the terrible siege of Vicksburg.

THE END

To follow another path, turn to page 121.
To read the conclusion, turn to page 211.

You hand the man the money. He gives you a slab of foul-smelling meat wrapped in old newspaper.

That night, you cook some of the meat, adding lots of spices in hopes you can forget what you're eating. Anna still refuses to eat the dog, but you choke it down. It tastes rotten. Less than an hour after you eat it, you're vomiting.

You feel weaker and weaker as the evening goes on. Anna helps you to bed, where you sleep restlessly. The next day, you're suffering from terrible diarrhea. You keep trying to vomit, but there's nothing left in your stomach. You feel burning hot one minute and cold the next.

The next thing you remember, an old doctor is standing over your bed. Anna is next to him, looking worried.

Turn the page.

It's days before you're well enough to get out of bed. Even then, you feel too weak to do anything. The shelling continues, and you realize that your house isn't safe. A few of your neighbors come over from the caves to help you and Anna move.

You spend several long, miserable weeks in the caves. On July 4, General Pemberton and the Confederate army surrender the city to General Grant's forces.

When you return home, your strength still hasn't returned. Anna, almost skeleton thin from the weeks of hunger, has to do the housework. You've survived the siege, but your body has paid a heavy price. You'll never be strong again.

THE END

To follow another path, turn to page 121.
To read the conclusion, turn to page 211.

"No, this doesn't feel right, Edward. Let's leave it alone."

Edward frowns. "That's what I get for going shell hunting with a couple of girls," he says. "I'll bring it back myself."

He bends over to lift the shell. "Don't!" you shout as you and Anna back up. Boom! The shell explodes as Edward lifts it. The sound is deafening. You scream as you're thrown to the ground. Anna is sobbing. "Edward's dead! He's dead!" she wails.

A small crowd gathers, rushing you and Anna away from the scene. A small piece of the shell hit your arm, and it's bleeding heavily. Back in the caves, an old woman tends to your wound. She serves you and Anna a thin, foul-tasting soup that you both eat without question. You realize that the little scraps of meat in the soup are rat, but you're too exhausted to care.

Turn the page.

On July 4, 1863, Grant's soldiers entered Vicksburg after Pemberton's surrender.

You and Anna survive by eating rat, mule, and whatever else you can find. On July 4, General Pemberton finally surrenders. The Yankees take control of the city. It's not the way you hoped it would end, but at least you can get food and clean water again.

208

You know the memory of young Edward will haunt you forever, but at least you're alive.

THE END

To follow another path, turn to page 121.
To read the conclusion, turn to page 211.

The caves are crawling with people. You and Anna find a small dugout and try to make it feel like home. The place smells terrible. Nobody has water to spare for bathing. The sounds of coughing and crying keep you up at night. It's a terrible way to live.

Anna adjusts better than you do. She proves to be an excellent rat trapper. The first time you cook and eat a rat, you both vomit. But after awhile, you get used to the idea and the taste. It's food, after all.

On July 4, General Pemberton surrenders. The Yankees take control of the city. You and Anna finally return home. But you know life in the South will never be the same.

THE END

To follow another path, turn to page 121.
To read the conclusion, turn to page 211.

President Lincoln (center) is shown with detective Allan Pinkerton (left) and General John McClernand (right) after the Battle of Antietam.

The Tide Turns

The Civil War was long and bloody. Early in the war, the Confederacy held the advantage. Confederate soldiers defeated the Union troops in battle after battle. Their victories included the first and second Battles of Bull Run and the Seven Days' Battles.

The Union army did have some success early on, including the bloody Battle of Antietam. Yet by the end of 1862, Confederate independence seemed like a real possibility. Northerners were tired of the war. Support for President Lincoln was fading. Many people believed political pressure could force the Union to give the Confederacy the independence it wanted.

The events of the spring and summer of 1863 were a turning point in the war. The change may have begun at Chancellorsville. Even though the Confederates won the battle, General Stonewall Jackson was killed. Jackson had been General Lee's most trusted officer. Without him, the Confederate army was never the same.

The loss of Jackson was strongly felt at Gettysburg. Lee lacked confidence in some of his generals. The Confederates failed to take the high ground that was so important to the battle. When General George Meade's force stopped Lee's final, desperate charge, the Union had the victory it so badly needed.

The fall of Vicksburg was even more important than Gettysburg. The Union then controlled the Mississippi River, splitting the Confederacy in two.

Union General William Sherman led the March to the Sea through Georgia.

The losses at Gettysburg and Vicksburg were a huge blow to the Confederates. Even so, they fought bravely for the next two years. The Confederacy had a few victories, but the Union had greater supplies and many more soldiers.

In 1864, Union General William Tecumseh Sherman captured the important railroad and factory town of Atlanta, Georgia. He then led his troops on a march through Georgia to Savannah. When Lincoln was elected again in 1864, the Confederacy's hopes were all but gone.

General Lee (right) surrendered to General Grant (left) on April 9, 1865.

After Vicksburg, Lincoln finally found the general he'd been looking for in Ulysses Grant. Grant had the confidence earlier Union generals had lacked. He wasn't afraid to attack, even if it meant losing men.

On April 9, 1865, Lee and Grant met in a small Virginia village called Appomattox Court House. There, Lee surrendered his army. In the following weeks, the other Confederate armies also surrendered. After four years of brutal, bloody war, it was over.

The Civil War left scars that lasted generations. Slavery ended, but life didn't improve greatly for African Americans. They were treated as second-class citizens for another 100 years, especially in the South. After the war, the federal government stepped in to govern the former Confederacy. This Reconstruction period lasted until 1877, when Southern states were again allowed to govern themselves.

The Civil War was perhaps the darkest time in American history. Neighbors, friends, and brothers fought against one another. More than 600,000 people died. But even with the problems the war caused, the country stayed together. We can only imagine how different our lives would be without the events of 1863.

TIME LINE

December 1860–June 1861 — Eleven Southern states secede from the Union to form the Confederate States of America.

April 12, 1861 — The Confederacy attacks Fort Sumter, South Carolina, beginning the Civil War.

July 21, 1861 — The Confederacy wins the war's first major battle at Bull Run, Virginia.

April 6–7, 1862 — The Union wins the Battle of Shiloh in Tennessee.

June 25–July 1, 1862 — The Confederacy wins the Seven Days' Battles near Richmond, Virginia.

September 17, 1862 — The Union wins the Battle of Antietam in Maryland.

May 1, 1863 — The heavy fighting of the Battle of Chancellorsville begins.

May 2, 1863 — General Stonewall Jackson is shot accidentally by his own troops.

May 6, 1863 — Union troops make their final retreat from Chancellorsville, giving the Confederacy the victory.

May 10, 1863 — Stonewall Jackson dies.

May 1863 — General Ulysses S. Grant begins the siege of Vicksburg.

July 1, 1863 — The Union and Confederate armies meet at Gettysburg.

July 3, 1863 — The final Confederate charge at Gettysburg fails; the Union wins the battle.

July 4, 1863 — General John Pemberton surrenders the city of Vicksburg to General Grant.

November 8, 1864 — President Lincoln is re-elected.

November 15, 1864 — General William Sherman begins his March to the Sea in Atlanta, Georgia.

December 10, 1864 — General Sherman's march reaches Savannah, Georgia. Savannah surrenders 11 days later.

April 9, 1865 — General Lee surrenders to General Grant at Appomattox Court House, Virginia.

April 15, 1865 — President Lincoln dies after being shot the evening before in Washington, D.C.

December 1865 — The 13th Amendment to the Constitution outlaws slavery in the United States.

1865 – 1877 — The federal government takes over Southern state governments; this period is called Reconstruction.

OTHER PATHS TO EXPLORE

In this book, you've seen how the events experienced by people during the Civil War look different from three points of view.

Perspectives on history are as varied as the people who lived it. You can explore other paths on your own to learn more about what happened. Seeing history from many points of view is an important part of understanding it.

Here are some ideas for other Civil War points of view to explore:

- ◆ Late in the war, many Southern families along Sherman's march feared that their homes would be burned down. What would that have been like?

- ◆ Friends and family members often fought on opposite sides. What would it have been like to meet a close friend, or even a brother, as an enemy on the battlefield?

- ◆ Some African Americans fought for the Union, but they were treated as second-class soldiers. What was the war like for them?

THE UNDERGROUND RAILROAD:

AN INTERACTIVE HISTORY ADVENTURE

BY ALLISON LASSIEUR

CONSULTANT:
PAUL BERNISH
NATIONAL UNDERGROUND RAILROAD FREEDOM CENTER
CINCINNATI, OHIO

TABLE OF CONTENTS

ABOUT YOUR ADVENTURE

YOU are living in the 1850s, wrestling with the question of slavery. Will you break the law to help slaves gain their freedom?

In this book, you'll explore how the choices people made meant the difference between freedom and enslavement, between success and failure. The events you'll experience happened to real people.

Chapter One sets the scene. Then you choose which path to read. Follow the directions at the bottom of each page. The choices you make will change your outcome. After you finish one path, go back and read the others for new perspectives.

YOU CHOOSE the path
you take through history.

Many slaves worked in cotton fields from dawn until dusk. They received no pay for their work.

THE SLAVERY QUESTION

It's the 1850s, and the United States is less than 100 years old. Immigrants have come from all over the world to settle in America. The streets of New York and Philadelphia are filled with the rumble and clatter of carriages, wagons, and horses. Factories and businesses in the North provide jobs for newcomers.

In the South, life is quiet and slow. Farmland stretches as far as anyone can see. Cotton and sugarcane make plantation owners rich.

There's something else different about the South. In the South, there are slaves.

Turn the page.

Slaves live every day knowing they are someone else's property. The food they eat, the clothing they wear, and even their own families are owned by someone else. For most slaves, it is the only life they will ever know. But some slaves run away. They risk everything, even their lives, for freedom.

You've heard of abolitionists in the North who think blacks and whites are equal. Some of them lead runaways through unfamiliar areas or hide them from slave catchers. Their routes are secret. But their network is growing. It's become known as the Underground Railroad. And there's more need for it now than ever.

An abolitionist in Pennsylvania built these sliding shelves to hide runaway slaves in a crawl space.

Runaways used to be safe if they made it to the North. But since the Fugitive Slave Act of 1850 was passed, slave owners can recapture slaves in any state. The only place slaves can truly be free now is Canada. And the act makes it illegal to help slaves escape.

Turn the page.

As an American living in the 1850s, you're not sure how you feel about that. You understand how important it is for slave owners to reclaim their property. How else would Southern plantation owners make a living?

Another part of you is uneasy at the idea of owning another human being. What if the abolitionists are right and all people are equal? Then slavery, and everything the South stands for, would be wrong. There are so many sides to this question, and there are no easy answers.

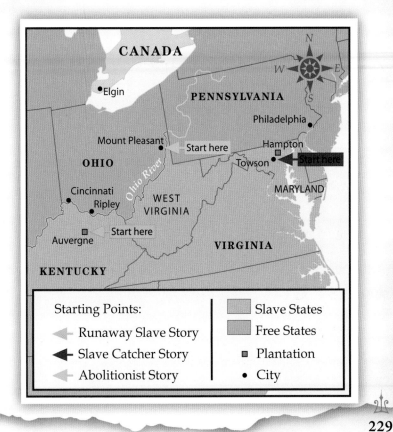

➤To experience what it's like to be a runaway slave, turn to page **231**.

➤If you want to see what it's like to be a slave catcher, turn to page **261**.

➤If you have the courage to break the law and be an abolitionist on the Underground Railroad, turn to page **293**.

Plantation owners had grand homes and large estates. Slaves worked in the gardens, the fields, and the big house.

CHAPTER 2

RUNNING TO FREEDOM

It's a beautiful spring morning in Kentucky. You're in one of the grand flower gardens that fill the yard around a large, beautiful home. The house is called Auvergne.

From the big house, you hear someone calling you. A knot of fear tightens in your stomach. You know that voice. It's the voice of your master, Brutus Clay. You are his slave.

You were born here. Your mother and father are also slaves. Your father works in the master's fields every day, from sunrise to sunset. Your mother works in the kitchen.

Turn the page.

"I want every flower bed weeded by sundown," Master Clay says to you. You have no choice, so you quickly get to work.

Hours later, your back aches and your hands are bleeding from pulling all the weeds. You glance back at the house as it grows dark. Through the window, you see Master Clay and his family sitting down to an elegant dinner.

You run toward the slave cabins. Black-eyed pea soup is bubbling in a pot over the fireplace. Your mother and father are talking frantically.

"Are you sure? How many of us will be sold?" your mother cries.

Sold? Your heart pounds and you can't breathe. Being sold away from your family is the worst thing imaginable.

Slaves lived in small cabins on their masters' plantations.

"I don't know how many," Father says. "But we can run before the slave trader comes."

"Run away? That's crazy talk! They'll hang us," your mother says.

"I have the money Master Clay let me keep when I worked on his neighbor's farm last fall," Father says. He stands up straight. "Better to die in freedom than live a slave. Come with me."

Turn the page.

Brutus Clay was the largest slaveholder in Kentucky.

Your mother refuses. Your baby brother is too little to travel, she says.

They come up with a plan. Master Clay is going to hire out Father to his neighbor again next week. Father will get a pass to travel to the other farm. That's when he'll escape. When he is free, he will earn enough money to buy the rest of the family.

Then they both look at you. "You're old enough to decide," Father says. "You can come with me. Or you can stay here with your mother."

What a terrible choice! If you go with your father, you risk being recaptured and sold. Or you could die in the wilderness. But you might make it to freedom. If you stay, you could help your mother. But you might be sold away from your family forever. What will you do?

➥ *If you choose to stay with your mother, turn to page 236.*

➥ *If you choose to flee with your father, turn to page 238.*

You can't leave your mother, no matter how sweet freedom sounds. Later that week, your father leaves. Three days pass before Master Clay realizes that your father isn't coming back. He sends for you and your mother.

"Where is he?" Master Clay demands.

"I don't know," your mother cries, shaking her head.

The next week, a slave trader comes to Auvergne. He speaks to Master Clay and hands him money. The slave trader chains your wrists.

"Come with me," he says roughly. You can hear your mother begging Master Clay not to sell you as you're thrown into the back of a wagon. The last thing you see is your poor mother collapsed in the dirt road, screaming and crying for you.

The stern man tells you he is the manager of a huge sugarcane plantation in Louisiana. For the rest of the trip, he makes you walk behind the wagon. At night, you have to sleep on the ground. It's cold, but the man doesn't give you a blanket.

Several days later, you arrive at the Mississippi River. You and several other slaves are chained together on the deck of a boat. Most of them don't talk much. Like you, they miss their families.

You lose track of the days. You and the rest of the slaves are forced to stay on the deck, no matter what the weather. Rain drenches you. The sun beats down, and there's no shade. Nights are cold. All you can do is sit on the deck with your head in your hands. The chains seem to grow heavier each hour.

Turn to page 240.

The pull of freedom is strong. You decide to go with your father. You make a plan. When your father gets permission to leave, he will wait for you in the woods a few miles down the road. After dark, you will join him. Then you'll both head north, toward the border of Kentucky and the free state of Ohio.

Slave tags like this one were required for slaves who traveled between plantations.

Two days later, Father comes to the cabin. He shows you a small metal tag hanging around his neck. It's his pass to leave Auvergne. You're scared and excited at the same time.

The next afternoon, Father leaves as expected. The hours until dark seem to drag by. Finally, all the lights in the big house go off. You slip out the door and run, keeping to the shadows. Soon you see your father's tall figure.

You and your father walk all night. Suddenly, a black man on horseback rounds the bend in the road.

→*If you choose to ask this man for help, turn to page 242.*

→*If you choose to move on alone and risk your life in the wilderness, turn to page 246.*

When the horrible river journey ends, you're loaded on another wagon. A short time later, the wagon turns around a bend in the road. Spread out in front of you is the largest farm you've ever seen. Miles of fields stretch in every direction. A large building stands near the fields. The huge sugar processing machines inside are rumbling and clattering. Overseers with their whips yell at groups of slaves to work harder.

The manager pulls you out of the wagon, and your legs collapse from fear and hunger. He hauls you up as a large man approaches.

"Here's the overseer of Ashland," the manager says to you. "Do what he says." He turns to the overseer. "Here's a new one for the fields."

Slaves likely helped build the great house at Ashland Plantation in Louisiana. It was completed in 1842.

The overseer takes the chains off and hands you over to another slave. "Get this one some food," he barks. He looks at you. "You'll start in the fields in the morning."

*Turn to page **244**.*

At first your heart thumps with fear. Then your father says, "I know him." Father speaks to the man. He shows the man his pass.

"He says he'll take us somewhere safe where we can rest," Father says. The man takes you through the woods to an isolated cabin. Your father tells him about the plan to escape to the North. You can only think of food and sleep.

When you get to the cabin, you open the door and tiredly stumble inside. Your father and the man are right behind you. The man slams the door and locks it behind you. Then he grabs you and pulls out a gun. It's a trap!

The man claps you both in chains, then throws you and Father in the back of a wagon. The man laughs. "You know the punishment for running away?" he sneers. "Master Clay could order up to 100 lashes with the whip!"

Slave catchers often set traps to catch runaway slaves.

Hope dies inside you. You could be whipped, too. You might even be hanged, as an example to other slaves of what happens when someone tries to escape. All you can do is hope that Master Clay will be kind to you when you return.

THE END

To follow another path, turn to page 229.
To read the conclusion, turn to page 319.

Even children had to work in the sugarcane fields. Overseers made sure slaves got the job done.

Two weeks have passed. Each morning, you go into the sugarcane fields with hundreds of other slaves. Your job is to hoe dirt over the sugarcane stalks after they are planted. You learned on the very first day that the dirt over the newly planted stalks must be exactly 3 inches deep.

The overseer saw you hoeing less dirt. He pulled out his whip and gave you five lashes. When you got up, the blood made your clothes stick to your skin. But you didn't dare stop or cry. You picked up your hoe and ran to catch up with the others. The blood dried on your back and made your clothes stiff and sticky.

At sundown, you walk to the cabin you share with several other slaves. There is no furniture. Every night as you fall asleep on the hard wood planks, you wonder what happened to your family. Did Father escape? Was Mother sold? You will probably never know. And they will likely never find out what happened to you. You have little chance of escape now.

THE END

To follow another path, turn to page 229.
To read the conclusion, turn to page 319.

"Do you trust him?" you ask your father.

"No," Father says. "Let's keep going." Father shows the man his pass. The man eyes it suspiciously and then rides away. You know he could be a slave catcher.

You and Father dash into the woods. It's well past daylight when you feel safe enough to stop. You drink from a small brook and then fall asleep under some bushes.

All day you rest in the woods. By evening, you feel stronger. You wait until the stars come out, and then Father points to the sky.

"See that group of stars that looks like a cup with a handle?" he asks. You nod. "It's called the Drinking Gourd. It points to the North Star—and to freedom."

Runaway slaves followed the Drinking Gourd, now called the Big Dipper, and the North Star to find their way.

Turn the page.

For days, you wander through the woods. There's always the danger of wild animals or a slave owner's dogs finding you. You're hungry all the time.

One night you reach the bank of a wide river. There's a bright light across the river. You just make out a house on top of a hill.

The village of Ripley, and freedom for runaway slaves, lay across the Ohio River.

"That land across the river is Ohio," Father says. "Freedom!" You can't believe that you're looking at a free state.

Along the shore you see a figure dressed in dark clothing and carrying a lantern. You and your father duck behind a large bush so you won't be seen.

As you look at the wide, cold river, your heart sinks. "How are we going to get across?" you whisper miserably.

Father stares at the river, and then looks at the man. "Looks like we have two choices," Father says finally. "Swim across, or ask that man for help."

➤If you choose to try to swim across the river, turn to page **252**.

➤If you choose to ask the man for help, turn to page **250**.

Slowly, you and your father approach the man, who's standing near a boat. To your surprise, you see that he's black.

"Welcome, friend," the man says. "We heard that there were two runaways in the woods nearby." He shakes Father's hand. "I'm John Parker. I'm a conductor on the Underground Railroad. My friend is waiting for us in the village of Ripley, on the other side of the river."

You all climb into the boat. On the other side, a white man helps you out.

"This is the Reverend John Rankin," Mr. Parker says. On a big hill in front of you is the house you saw from across the river. You climb 100 steps to the house.

The steps to John Rankin's house were climbed by many escaped slaves.

Go to page **253**.

"We have to swim across," Father says finally. "The water is cold, but we can do it!"

You're afraid of the big river, but you're more afraid of getting caught. You both quietly wade into the water. It's freezing! The current is very strong, but you're a strong swimmer. So is Father. You're so close to freedom!

As soon as you start swimming, you realize this was a big mistake. The river is much wider and stronger than you thought. You're too weak from hunger, fear, and weeks of travel to keep swimming. You feel yourself being dragged down. The last sight you see is your father's head bobbing in the water. You join the many slaves who died on their way to freedom.

THE END

To follow another path, turn to page 229.
To read the conclusion, turn to page 319.

A white woman with a kind face welcomes you. "Come in," she says, "I'm Jean Rankin." Soon you and Father are eating warm stew and fresh bread. No food has ever tasted better.

"My house has been the door to freedom for many human beings," Reverend Rankin says. "Tonight you can sleep in safety."

You curl up under a blanket beside the fire and fall asleep peacefully.

Reverend John Rankin helped more than 3,000 slaves escape while living in Ripley, Ohio.

Turn the page.

John Rankin's house stood on the highest point of a hill overlooking the Ohio River.

The next day, Reverend Rankin and Father discuss where you should go. "It's not safe for you to stay here," Reverend Rankin says.

"Isn't Ohio a free state?" you ask.

"Yes, but the Fugitive Slave Act lets slave catchers come into free states and recapture runaway slaves," Reverend Rankin explains.

"Then what should we do?" you ask.

"You could go to Cincinnati. It's a huge city with a large black population. Many former slaves live and work there. Or you could go to Canada. Slavery is illegal in the whole country. Your father can buy land and own his own farm in Canada."

Father's eyes light up at the idea. "I would love to have my own farm," he says. "But I also need to get a job now so I can make enough money to buy my wife and baby. I miss them so!"

"Mr. Parker and I will help you, no matter what you choose," Reverend Rankin replies.

➤If you choose to go to Cincinnati, turn to page 256.

➤If you choose to travel on to Canada, turn to page 258.

Cincinnati is about 50 miles away. That night, you go to Mr. Parker's house. You and Father get into a wagon, and Mr. Parker hides you among boxes.

Mr. Parker takes you to a small church, where several black people are there to meet you. Mr. Parker tells you that this is a black church. The church members help the Underground Railroad. A kind black woman gives you and Father food and a warm bed. The next night, another church member takes you to Cincinnati.

When you reach Cincinnati, you're taken to the home of Samuel and Sally Wilson. They give you a safe place to stay for the night. "We know many people who can help you," the Wilsons assure you.

Cincinnati was a destination for many runaway slaves.

Abolitionists in Cincinnati help Father find a job and a place to live. Here, you hope to blend in with the huge black population of the city. You try to breathe easier. Maybe you're free at last.

257

THE END

To follow another path, turn to page 229.
To read the conclusion, turn to page 319.

You realize that in Canada, you will never fear being recaptured. Reverend Rankin and Mr. Parker arrange for you and Father to take a train to Canada.

After a long train ride, you reach Toronto. There, you meet several free blacks who tell you about a settlement called Elgin. It is a community made up mainly of runaway slaves. At Elgin, your father buys a small farm with the money Reverend Rankin gave him. Soon he's planting his own crops. You go to school for the first time in your life. Even more amazing, some of your classmates are white!

For the first time in the weeks since you left Auvergne, you feel truly free. If you and Father work hard and save money, someday you can buy your mother and little brother. You'll bring them to Canada, the place that former slaves call "The Promised Land."

THE END

To follow another path, turn to page 229.
To read the conclusion, turn to page 319.

$100 REWARD!

RANAWAY

From the undersigned, living on Current River, about twelve miles above Doniphan, in Ripley County, Mo., on 2nd of March, 1860, A NF GRO MAN, about 30 years old, weighs about 160 pounds; high forehead, with a scar on it; had on brown pants and coat very much worn, and an old black wool hat; shoes size No. 11.

The above reward will be given to any person who may apprehend this said negro out of the State; and fifty dollars if apprehended in this State outside of Ripley county, or $25 if taken in Ripley county.

APOS TUCKER.

Slave owners offered rewards for the return of their slaves.

CHAPTER 3

SLAVE CATCHER: ON THE HUNT

All your life you've lived on a small farm near the town of Towson, Maryland. Your family has always been poor. A few months back, a local plantation owner asked if you would find one of his runaway slaves. He couldn't spare his overseer to look for the runaway. You found the runaway hiding in the woods, and the owner gave you a reward. You realized that you could make a lot of money catching slaves.

Turn the page.

One day, you read notices in the newspaper about runaway slaves. One of them catches your eye. It's from Mr. Ridgely, who owns a nearby plantation called Hampton. Maybe he would hire you.

That same day, you see a notice tacked up at the store. The notice offers a $50 reward for the capture of a young black woman named Mary. She's run away from a plantation in Virginia.

You could look for either one of these runaways. There's a reward for the return of the girl. But sometimes plantation owners offer extras, like payment for expenses. You stand to make a nice profit either way. Which slave do you decide to try to find?

→ *If you go visit Mr. Ridgely at Hampton, turn to page* **265**.

→ *If you set out to find the girl, go to page* **263**.

You think that finding the girl won't be too much trouble. The notice says that she was recently sold to a nearby farmer.

You search the area for several days. Finally, you spot a camp in the woods. That night, you hide and wait. Sure enough, after dark a short young woman appears. You step out of your hiding place, pistol drawn.

"Mary?" you ask with a grin. "I've been looking for you."

Mary's face falls. Tears well up in her eyes. "Don't shoot me, sir," she pleads. "I'll come with no fuss. My mistress will give you a reward for me."

Turn the page.

The sign said the reward was $50. That's more than you make as a farmer in a year. But you know that some slaves are worth far more than that at auction. Especially young female slaves like Mary. You could return her to her owner, knowing that you'd get the reward. Or you could gamble that you'll make more if you sell her yourself.

➤To return Mary for the reward money, turn to page **268**.

➤To sell her yourself, turn to page **274**.

Hampton was owned by several generations of the Ridgely family.

When you arrive at Hampton, you're shown into a huge room filled with expensive furniture.

"I hear you have a runaway slave," you say to Mr. Ridgely when he comes in.

"Yes. Henry Jones. He's one of my favorites," Mr. Ridgely replies. He describes Henry as 5 feet, 9 inches tall, light skinned, with full lips and a lean face.

Turn the page.

John Ridgely owned Hampton in the mid-1800s. He had about 60 slaves, including Henry Jones.

"When did he go missing?" you ask.

"A few weeks ago."

You frown. You know that the longer a slave has been gone, the less likely he'll be found. But you're determined to try. "I can find him for you," you say.

"If you find him within the county, I'll pay you $50. If you find him outside the county, I'll double it," Mr. Ridgely says. He also agrees to pay your expenses, which you tell him are 6 cents a mile and $2 a day. You shake hands on the deal.

Now, where do you look? Henry has been gone so long, he's probably not anywhere nearby. Maybe someone local saw Henry before he left. Pennsylvania is the nearest free state. You've heard of the Underground Railroad helping runaways make it to Philadelphia.

➜*If you decide to ask around town, turn to page 269.*

➜*If you go to Philadelphia, turn to page 285.*

"Come on," you say gruffly. You tie Mary's hands and lead her back to your house. The next day, you put her in the back of your wagon and start out for her owner's farm. The trip will take at least a week, but you don't mind. You know that there will be a reward for you.

You and Mary travel every day. At night you stop and make camp. You chain Mary to the wagon so she won't escape. The third night out, you're awakened by a noise. Slowly, you draw your pistol and peer into the dark woods beyond your camp. You hear a slight rustling noise. It could be a deer. Or it could be something else.

➤ If you choose to investigate the noise, turn to page **278**.

➤ If you choose to roll over and go back to sleep, turn to page **271**.

No one around town has seen a slave that matches Henry's description. You decide to ask the local patrollers. If anyone knows about runaways in the area, it would be them.

Patrols are groups of men who ride everywhere, looking for slaves. You thought about joining a patrol, but decided against it. Patrollers don't get paid, and you wanted to make some money.

The storekeeper is one of the patrollers. "We caught a male slave a few days ago. Arrested him for stealing a chicken," the storekeeper says. His description of the man doesn't quite match Mr. Ridgely's description. It could be Henry, though.

"What happened to the slave?" you ask the storekeeper.

Turn the page.

"We threw him in the county jail," the man replies. "He's probably still there."

"No," a man in the store pipes up. "He escaped before the patrol could get him into the jail. I hear he's hiding out in the woods a few miles from here."

"I'm sure they put him in the jail," the storekeeper insists. "I saw him there myself."

Great. Now what do you do?

➼If you choose to go to the jail, turn to page **272**.

➼If you choose to search the woods, turn to page **277**.

The next morning you awake. Mary is gone! The chain on the wagon is still there. The lock on the metal cuff is broken. Cursing, you look everywhere. But you know that Mary is long gone. She could have gone in any direction. You decide not to go after her.

Reluctantly, you turn your wagon around and start home. On the way, you wonder if Mr. Ridgely still needs someone to find his runaway slave Henry. Cheered by the thought, you start to whistle. Slave catchers always have work, and you're sure to find more.

THE END

To follow another path, turn to page 229.
To read the conclusion, turn to page 319.

Once Harriet Tubman escaped slavery, she risked her life to free other slaves.

At the jail, the sheriff confirms that the patrol brought in a slave last week.

"Can I see him, please?" you ask. "I'm looking for one of Mr. Ridgley's runaways."

"He escaped two days ago," the sheriff says.

"Did you look for him?" you ask.

"Why should I?" the sheriff says. "He ain't getting far around here. Either the patrol will catch him, or he'll starve to death in the woods."

"Either that," the sheriff continues, "or he was helped by that Harriet Tubman."

You've heard of Harriet Tubman. She's a former slave. Now she works as a conductor on the Underground Railroad. Rumor says that she travels between Maryland and Philadelphia, helping runaways to freedom. If Harriet Tubman helped Henry, he's as good as gone. But you're not willing to give up yet.

Going to the jail was a waste of time. Or was it? If the escaped prisoner was Henry, you know he's only had a two day head start. If it wasn't, you may be on a big wild goose chase.

➤If you decide to check the woods for Henry, turn to page 277.

➤If you think Henry escaped north and you decide to head to Philadelphia, turn to page 285.

The trip to Mary's plantation will take too long, you think. It could be days, maybe weeks, before you get the reward. It's better if you sell her yourself.

Two days later, a crowd gathers at the auction house. One by one, each slave is brought onto a stage. The buyers poke and prod them. They pinch the slaves to see how strong their muscles are. The white men put grubby hands into the slaves' mouths, inspecting their teeth. They make the slaves run, march, and jump up and down.

When Mary is brought up, the auctioneer says, "This is Mary. She's low in stature but well-proportioned, of strong and healthy appearance, and of dark copper color."

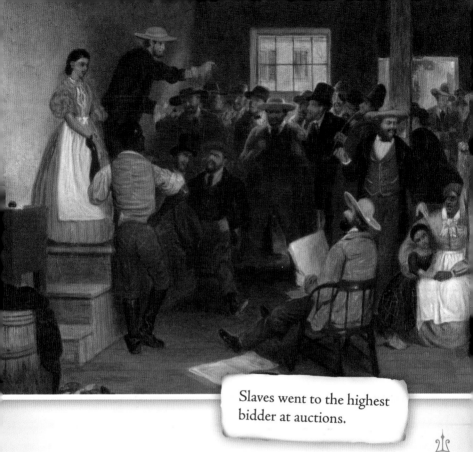

Slaves went to the highest bidder at auctions.

The bidding gets lively, with three men competing to buy her. When the gavel comes down, Mary is sold for $200. As she is led away, you're given $100, your share of the sale.

Turn the page.

The auctioneer approaches you. "She was a fine specimen," the man says. "If you get any more like her, bring them here. I'll make sure they sell for a good price."

You smile. You'll be back. There will always be other slaves.

THE END

To follow another path, turn to page 229.
To read the conclusion, turn to page 319.

The next day, you ride all over the county, through the woods where slaves might be hiding. Near a road, you see a black figure crouching behind a tree.

"What are you doing there?" you ask.

"I'm running an errand for my master . . . um, Mr. Stanley," the boy says. His voice is shaking.

You know Mr. Stanley. "He doesn't own any youngsters," you reply.

"He just bought me last week," the boy says.

"Okay, then, show me your pass." You know that slaves must have a pass to travel off the plantation.

"I lost it," the boy says. He starts to cry.

➤*If you choose to let the boy go, turn to page **280**.*
➤*If you choose to take the boy prisoner, turn to page **282**.*

Slowly, you get up and sneak into the woods. It must be a deer, you think. Then you hear a thin cough.

"Stop!" you shout, pointing your pistol at the noise. "I'll shoot! Identify yourself!"

"Don't hurt me," a voice says. It's Mary.

You grab her arm and drag her back to camp. You examine the chain that held her to the wagon. The lock on the metal cuff is broken.

Chains were used to keep slaves from running away while they were being transported.

Grumbling, you fish two chains and cuffs out of the back of your wagon. You put one on Mary's wrist. The other one goes on Mary's ankle. Then you attach them both to the wagon in such a way that Mary is forced to stand up all night.

"Maybe this will teach you not to run," you say gruffly. Tears roll down Mary's cheeks. You ignore them. "And no food for you tomorrow." You know that a hungry and exhausted slave is less likely to try to escape.

Turn to page 281.

You're pretty sure the boy is lying. But you don't have time to deal with him. Besides, he's a kid. He could be telling the truth. And if he's running away, he won't get far.

"Get out of here, boy," you say gruffly. "If I ever see you out alone again I'll whip you myself."

"Yes, yes!" the boy shouts as he runs down the road. "Thank you, thank you."

As you watch him, you think that you could have sold him yourself and made some money. But Henry is the bigger prize. Tomorrow you'll head for Philadelphia. Maybe you'll have better luck there.

Turn to page 285.

You don't have any more trouble. Three days later, you arrive at the plantation.

As you drive up, a little girl yells, "Mama, Mama!" Mary jumps out of the wagon, and the girl grabs her neck, hugging her tightly.

"My baby, my baby!" Mary weeps. "I didn't think I'd ever see you again."

A white woman appears. "Did you find my Mary?" she asks. "I'm so glad! I was having such a time training Ruth to clean the floors just so!"

The woman turns to Mary. "How dare you put us in such a bind, you worthless girl," she scolds. "And only a week before our big party! How could you be so uncaring?" Mary bows her head and says nothing.

Turn to page 284.

Slaves had little but the clothes on their back when they escaped.

"Well, we'll see about that," you say. You clap the boy in chains and take him to the jail.

"I found this one in the woods outside of town while I was looking for Henry Jones," you say. "Says Josiah Stanley is his master."

"Stanley don't own no kids," the sheriff says. "Boy, where are you really from?"

Crying, he admits that he's from a plantation in Virginia. He got lost trying to find his mother, who was sold a few weeks ago.

The sheriff puts the boy in a jail cell. He writes a letter to the boy's owner in Virginia. If the owner comes for the boy, the sheriff will get the reward money. If not, he can sell the boy.

As you leave the jail, the sheriff stops you. "I heard talk of a group of abolitionists from Philadelphia who come down here to help runaway slaves. That Henry you're looking for might be in their company."

"Thank you," you say. "I had thought to try Philadelphia next."

Turn to page 285.

You clear your throat. "Um, ma'am, I'm here for the reward," you say.

"Of course!" the woman replies. She pulls out a small purse. "There's $50 in gold coins. Thank you so much for bringing back my Mary." Then she takes Mary roughly by the arm into the house.

You get into your wagon and head for home. This reward will buy food and clothing for your family for several months. And there will always be other slaves to find.

THE END

To follow another path, turn to page 229.
To read the conclusion, turn to page 319.

It's dangerous being a slave catcher in Philadelphia. The Fugitive Slave Act makes it legal for you to go there and recapture runaway slaves. But many abolitionists in the city help runaway slaves. And they hate slave catchers. You'll have to be careful.

When you arrive, you spend days watching known Underground Railroad stations like the Johnson House. You hire a black informant to spy on William Still. You know he hides runaway slaves at his home on South Street.

Turn the page.

William Still helped escaped slaves who came to Philadelphia.

One day, your informant tells you he saw a black man who looks like Henry at Still's home. You start watching his house yourself. Sure enough, one night a tall black man leaves the house with several other men. He looks like Henry, but you're not sure.

It's too dangerous for you to confront them alone. A mob of abolitionists would likely tear you apart! But that black man really looked like Henry. You could follow the men to see where they go. Or, you could take the safe route by returning to Maryland and telling Mr. Ridgely that his slave is lost.

➤*If you follow the men, turn to page **288**.*
➤*If you return to Maryland, turn to page **290**.*

It's dark, so the men don't notice you following them. They go into a building downtown. This must be where William Still's abolitionist group meets. You watch the building.

An hour later, the black man comes out—alone! You can't believe your luck. You walk across the street.

"Henry Jones?" you ask politely.

The man turns. In a flash, you realize it's not Henry after all. But maybe you can capture this one and sell him. You quickly pull out a set of shackles and try to slap them on the man's wrists.

"Help!" he yells. "A slave catcher!"

The door bursts open, and men pour into the street. Suddenly you're surrounded.

Panicked, you push through the crowd and race down the street. The mob roars behind you, but you don't dare look back. You dash through alleys, hiding in the maze of streets. The sound behind you dies down, and you stop, gasping for breath.

You lost them.

You're lucky to have escaped. You limp back to your carriage and head out of town. Mr. Ridgely might be angry you couldn't find Henry, but there's nothing more you can do.

Turn the page.

You go back to Maryland and tell Mr. Ridgely your story. "I'm disappointed," Mr. Ridgely says. "Henry was one of my most trusted boys. I just don't understand why he'd leave such a good life here. But it sounds like he's not coming back."

"Thank you for your work," he continues, paying you for your expenses.

"You know, sir," you say, "If you had hired me sooner, I might have been able to find Henry before he got too far."

"You're right," Mr. Ridgely replies.
"I shouldn't have waited so long to hire you.
I thought Henry would come back in a few
days. They usually do. Next time I'll contact
you straight away."

You nod. You know that there will be
plenty of work from Mr. Ridgely and other
slave owners in the area.

THE END

To follow another path, turn to page 229.
To read the conclusion, turn to page 319.

The Free Labor Store in Mount Pleasant, Ohio, refused to sell goods made by slave labor.

CHAPTER 4

THE ABOLITIONISTS' STORY

You've always believed slavery is wrong, but not everyone agrees with you. You belong to the Society of Friends, also called Quakers. This religious group thinks slavery is wrong. But some Quakers think it's wrong to break the law to help slaves. You are not one of them.

You decide to move to an area where you can help runaway slaves. You buy a farm outside the small town of Mount Pleasant, Ohio. Many townspeople there are against slavery. There's even a Free Labor Store that will not sell anything made by slave labor.

293

Turn the page.

David Updegraff was part of the Underground Railroad in Mount Pleasant.

One day you meet a gentleman named David Updegraff. You've heard that Updegraff is very active in the Underground Railroad. Some people say that he's helped dozens of runaway slaves.

"Good morning, friend," he says pleasantly. "Are you settling in?"

"Yes, I feel at home here," you reply.

"I'm glad to be among people who have the same anti-slavery feelings I do."

"Good, good," Updegraff says. Then he pauses. "As you well know, many of us here in Mount Pleasant are part of the Underground Railroad," he says gravely.

"How can I help?" you ask.

"Thank you for your offer," Updegraff replies. "We need conductors who can take slaves to other stations on the Underground Railroad. We also need a stationmaster who could house and feed slaves when they pass through town. Which one would you like to do?"

➤ *If you choose to become a conductor, turn to page **296**.*

➤ *If you choose to become a stationmaster, turn to page **299**.*

"Excellent!" Mr. Updegraff says. "We'll be in touch when we have slaves who need transport."

Three days later, you receive a strange note. It says, "I have three horses for sale: a stallion, a mare, and a foal. If interested, please visit my barn tomorrow night. If you do not want these horses, I will ask Mr. Daniel Hise of Salem if he is willing to take them." The note is signed "D. Updegraff."

The note is in code! But you figure out what it means. Three slaves are on their way. You are to meet Mr. Updegraff at his farm tomorrow night and take them to Mr. Hise, the next stop on the railroad.

When you arrive, Mr. Updegraff takes you to the barn. There, huddled in the shadows, are three slaves: a father, mother, and their 6-year-old son. They look at you with fear and hope.

Wagons with hidden compartments were used to secretly transport escaped slaves.

"You're safe now," you say. You and Mr. Updegraff show them a secret compartment in your wagon. They crawl into it and you carefully close the door. You pile hay on top to hide the compartment.

Turn the page.

At last, everything is ready for you to leave. You're excited and afraid. If a slave catcher finds you, you could be arrested.

The first few hours go by quickly. Then, as you round a bend, you see a man standing in the road. He signals at you to stop. You've never seen this man before. You get uneasy. Is this a trap?

→ If you stop and talk to the man, turn to page **300**.

→ If you choose to drive on, turn to page **308**.

You put a lighted lantern in the window every night so runaways know your home is a safe house. A few nights later, you get a knock on the door, very late. It's Updegraff. He leads two young black men wearing tattered clothing into your house. Their names are John and David. They're exhausted and terrified. But they also have the light of freedom in their eyes.

"You're free now," you say. "Have some food and be comfortable."

After they eat, you give them each a new set of clothes. "Now I feel really free," John says. "These are my first clothes as a free man."

You lead them to the barn, where they will sleep for the night. Just as you are starting to fall asleep, you hear another knock. At the door is a black man you've never seen before.

Turn to page 302.

Daniel Hise lived in Salem, Ohio, north of Mount Pleasant.

You slow the wagon to a stop.

"Are you Mr. Updegraff's friend? The one who is buying the horses?" the man asks.

"Why do you want to know?" you reply.

"I am Daniel Hise," the man says. "I am anxious to have the horses in my possession. I have heard there are horse thieves out tonight!"

Slave catchers! You nod and motion for Hise to get into the wagon. "They are safe in the back," you whisper.

"Good, we must hurry," Hise says. You drive your horses as fast as they can go, hoping that you make it to Hise's farm before daybreak.

No such luck. Just a short way down the road, a gang of slave catchers with guns blocks the way.

"Stop!" one of them shouts. "Stop now, I say!"

➼If you decide to stop and let them search the wagon, turn to page **303**.

➼If you decide to turn around and try to run, turn to page **309**.

"Please, sir, let me in," the man begs. "I've got slave catchers on my tail!"

You are immediately suspicious. Sometimes slave catchers set traps like this to catch people helping runaways. But if this man is a runaway, he'll be in danger if you turn him away. What do you do?

➤If you choose to open the door, turn to page **306**.

➤If you choose to tell the man to go away, turn to page **312**.

Your heart thumps as you slow the wagon to a stop. The slave catchers swarm the wagon. "I know you, Hise," one slave catcher says. "Are you hiding runaways?"

"No, sir," Hise says smoothly. "I've been on my friend's farm, helping with chores."

"This time of night?" one slave catcher sneers. Any minute, you think, they'll find the secret compartment.

"Of course not," Hise replies. "We worked until dark and my friend kindly gave me food and a bed. But I've got my own chores, so I need to get back early."

Turn the page.

You hold your breath. Amazingly, they seem to believe Hise's story. The leader motions to the men, who move away from the wagon. You sigh in relief. You and Hise watch as the gang rides away. As soon as they're out of earshot, you tap on the floor of the wagon.

"Are you all right?" you ask softly. You hear a light tap in reply.

Daniel Hise's house in Salem, Ohio, had secret rooms under the house where he could hide runaways.

You race to Hise's farm. Then you help the runaways out of the wagon and into the house.

"I have a secret room where you can stay for a few days," Hise says to the fugitives. "When you're rested, we'll get you to the next safe house further north."

You stay and rest, too. You'll return to your farm tomorrow, ready to help the next group of runaway slaves.

THE END

To follow another path, turn to page 229.
To read the conclusion, turn to page 319.

You can't turn the man away. But just as you open the door, several white men with guns appear out of the darkness. It's a trap!

The men push their way into your home. Shouting, they destroy everything in your house. The furniture is thrown into the yard and set on fire. Your clothing is tossed into the trees. All your food is thrown into the dirt.

"Where are they?" one man yells, pointing a rifle at your head. When you don't answer, he pushes the gun into your ear and says, "If you turn them over to us, we won't kill you."

You're terrified. But you continue to insist that you are not hiding slaves. The gang searches the rest of the house and the barn, but find nothing. The runaways must have heard the commotion and gotten away, you think with much relief.

The slave catchers finally leave, but everything in your house is destroyed. Strangely, as you look at the damage, you're not angry. Instead, this attack makes you more determined than ever to fight slavery.

THE END

To follow another path, turn to page 229.
To read the conclusion, turn to page 319.

The only safe thing you can think of is to drive past the stranger. As you do, he yells at you to stop. "I'm waiting for someone who is looking to buy some horses," the man says. "Would that be you?"

"Perhaps," you reply nervously. "Who are you and why do you want to know?"

"I'm Daniel Hise," the man says. "Updegraff told me to find you," he says. "He got word that there are horse thieves on the roads tonight. It's not safe to complete the transaction now."

You hesitate. How do you know this isn't a trap? "You must trust me," he says. "Either turn around and go back, or follow me into the woods."

➜ If you choose to turn around and go home,
turn to page **315**.

➜ If you decide to follow Hise, turn to page **316**.

Slave catchers attack a wagon of escaped slaves.

You feel the panic rise in your chest. Now that they've seen you, your only chance is to run, you think. You turn the wagon around as quickly as you can.

You push the horses as fast as they can go. The slave catchers give chase, yelling "Stop!" and shooting their guns in the air. Your heavy wagon will never outrun them, so you finally stop.

Turn the page.

The slave catchers swarm onto the wagon. It's not long before they find the secret compartment.

"So, what's this?" the leader asks, jabbing the runaways with the butt of his rifle. The men grab you and Hise and throw you in the back of your wagon along with the three runaways. The slave catchers tie you up and drive back to Mount Pleasant. Soon you find yourself in a bare jail cell with Hise. You've been arrested under the Fugitive Slave Act.

The day of your trial comes. The courtroom is packed with friends, family, and neighbors from Mount Pleasant. The evidence is presented. The trial is short, because you admit to helping the runaways.

"Guilty!" the judge says and he sentences you to 30 days in jail and a $500 fine. You are quickly hustled away to the jail.

You know the time will pass. It's a small price to pay for helping slaves escape. You hear that the family was broken up and all three—even the little boy—were sold away. The news makes you even more determined to continue your work once you get out of jail.

THE END

To follow another path, turn to page 229.
To read the conclusion, turn to page 319.

Slaves' clothing was often tattered and torn by the time they arrived in the North.

You tell the man to go away. He begs you again—the slave catchers are right behind him! If they find the others in the barn, you'll all be killed. Quickly, you think of a plan. You put on the man's threadbare coat and hat. Then you send him to the barn to warn the others.

You run to the road and start walking slowly. Soon a gang of slave catchers appears.

"Stop!" they yell. "Who are you? Why are you here so late at night?"

"I'm passing through," you say casually. "I'm on my way to Salem, and I'm anxious to get home."

The men look at your shabby clothing and laugh. But one stares at you. "So you've been on the road for hours?"

"Yes," you reply.

"Then you must have seen a runaway slave who came by here a little while ago."

"Why yes, I did see a black man a few miles back," you say, thinking quickly. "Said he was free, though. He was going to Cincinnati to find work."

Turn the page.

After a few more questions, they seem satisfied and leave. When you're sure they've gone, you run home. The runaways are still huddled in the barn with the man, terrified.

"It's no longer safe for you here," you say. "The slave catchers are gone, but they might come back."

The next morning you send a coded message to Updegraff. "I cannot take the horses you offered," you write. "There are too many horse thieves in town these days."

At dawn the next day, Updegraff arrives with a wagon and takes the runaways to the next station on the Underground Railroad.

THE END

To follow another path, turn to page 229.
To read the conclusion, turn to page 319.

"I'll go back home," you tell Hise. "I'll keep the horses in my barn tonight," you say.

"Good," Hise says. "Make sure they stay out of sight. I'll contact you when it's safe."

You drive home slowly, so as to not arouse suspicion. Thankfully, you don't see anyone on the road. For the next week, you live in fear that the runaways will be discovered.

A few days later, you receive word from Hise that it's safe to try again. That night you load the family into the wagon and make your way to Hise's farm. This time, you arrive safely. Even though this adventure is over, you know there will be another one soon.

THE END

To follow another path, turn to page 229.
To read the conclusion, turn to page 319.

Swampy, wooded areas were good hiding places for slaves trying to escape.

When you get safely into the woods, you and Hise open the secret compartment. The runaways look terrified.

The woman lays a trembling hand on your sleeve. "Thank you," she says softly. "Thank you for saving us tonight."

For the first time, the importance of what you're doing hits you. These are not just runaways. They're people, with hopes, dreams, and fears just like yours.

You unhitch the horses. Quickly you put the runaways on horseback and plunge deeper into the woods. Hours later, near dawn, you arrive at a small shack near the edge of a swampy area. You and Hise help the exhausted runaways bed down for a few hours of sleep.

You realize that it might be too dangerous for you to go back to your house. You decide to stay here until the slave catchers have left and then return home.

THE END

To follow another path, turn to page 229.
To read the conclusion, turn to page 319.

Harriet Tubman is pictured on the left, with several of the former slaves she helped bring to freedom.

CHAPTER 5

THE END OF THE UNDERGROUND RAILROAD

The Underground Railroad helped an estimated 70,000 to 100,000 slaves escape between the 1830s and the start of the Civil War in 1861. Every year more people joined the Underground Railroad to work as spies, informants, stationmasters, and conductors.

Conductors such as Harriet Tubman, a former slave, sneaked into slave states to guide runaways to freedom. In some cases, slaves on farms and plantations worked as conductors. They put themselves in great danger to help their fellow slaves escape.

Stationmasters, such as John and Jean Rankin, housed slaves in their homes. Often whole families supported Underground Railroad efforts. Levi and Catherine Coffin always had their home in Newport, Indiana, ready for escaped slaves who might come there.

Levi Coffin gave escaped slaves a place to rest in his Indiana home.

Slave owners and Southern politicians didn't sit back and let all this happen. Slaves were a big investment for their owners. Cotton and sugar were the basis of the Southern economy. Without slavery, the huge plantations couldn't function. To plantation owners, slavery was necessary. Politicians passed local and state laws to control slavery and keep the slaves from running. Slave catchers roamed everywhere, looking for fugitives.

Tension over slavery kept growing. In Congress, senators from Northern states fought and argued with Southern senators. Southerners were convinced they had the right to govern themselves as they wanted. If they wanted to keep slaves, they insisted, it was no one's business. Northerners didn't agree.

In 1860, Northerner Abraham Lincoln was elected president. Southern states saw his election as a defeat for themselves and their desires for self-government. Beginning with South Carolina, 11 states seceded from the Union. They formed their own nation, the Confederate States of America. Lincoln said that these states had no right to secede. This disagreement led to the Civil War.

The start of the Civil War led even more slaves to try to escape. In 1863, President Lincoln signed the Emancipation Proclamation, which freed all slaves living in states that had seceded. Slaves fled the South by the tens of thousands. Many former slaves became soldiers for the Union. By the end of the war, slavery had all but ended. In 1865, the 13th Amendment to the Constitution ended slavery for good.

This group of freed slaves worked with the 13th Massachusetts Infantry Regiment during the Civil War.

The need for the Underground Railroad was gone. The abolitionists who had worked so hard to end slavery now focused their efforts on helping newly freed slaves.

At a huge rally in Cincinnati, Levi Coffin announced the end of the Underground Railroad. He said, "Our underground work is done, and as we have no more use for the road, I would suggest that the rails be taken up and disposed of."

TIME LINE

1793—The first Fugitive Slave Act is passed, stating that slaves must be returned to their owners.

1822—Reverend John Rankin moves to Ripley, Ohio, and begins helping slaves escape.

1835–1850—Slave Henry Jones appears in records at Hampton.

1845—Brutus Clay of Bourbon County, Kentucky, reports owning 57 slaves.

1849—John Parker moves to Ripley, Ohio.

1850—The Fugitive Slave Act of 1850 allows slaveholders to retrieve slaves in Northern states and free territories, and makes it illegal to help runaway slaves.

1850—An advertisement for runaway slave Henry Jones appears in the local newspaper. Henry Jones never returns to Hampton.

1850–1860—Harriet Tubman makes 19 trips into Maryland to free about 300 slaves.

1860—Abraham Lincoln is elected president of the United States. South Carolina secedes from the Union.

1861—The Civil War begins after Confederate forces fire on Fort Sumter.

1863—Abraham Lincoln signs the Emancipation Proclamation, which frees slaves in the Confederate states. Many freed slaves fight for the North in the Civil War.

1865—The Civil War ends and the 13th Amendment to the U.S. Constitution outlaws slavery.

1870—The 15th Amendment gives African American men the right to vote.

OTHER PATHS TO EXPLORE

In this book, you've seen how events surrounding the Underground Railroad look different from three points of view.

Perspectives on history are as varied as the people who lived it. You can explore other paths on your own to learn more about what happened. Seeing history from many points of view is an important part of understanding it.

Here are some ideas for other Underground Railroad points of view to explore:

♦ Plantation owners in the 1800s depended on slaves to get their farm work done. What was it like to own slaves?

♦ Besides helping fugitive slaves, abolitionists published articles and gave speeches to convince others that slavery was wrong. What was it like to try to change something that many people favored?

♦ Abraham Lincoln was not in favor of abolishing slavery at the beginning of the Civil War. What things happened to change his mind?